Christian Footings

Creation, World Religions, Personalism,
Revelation, and Jesus

Revised Edition

University Press of America,® Inc.
Lanham · Boulder · New York · Toronto · Plymouth, UK

Copyright © 2009 by
University Press of America,® Inc.
4501 Forbes Boulevard
Suite 200
Lanham, Maryland 20706
UPA Acquisitions Department (301) 459-3366

Estover Road
Plymouth PL6 7PY
United Kingdom

Library of Congress Control Number: 2009931144
ISBN-13: 978-0-7618-4786-1 (paperback : alk. paper)
ISBN-10: 0-7618-4786-3 (paperback : alk. paper)
eISBN-13: 978-0-7618-4787-8
eISBN-10: 0-7618-4787-1

Contents

Anthology

Preface to the Revised Edition

Christian Footings has enjoyed some popularity, and I wanted to update parts of it, especially the section on Jesus. This book can serve as a framework for fundamental theology as well as an introduction to key Christian authors. One of my great professors at Fordham, John Heaney, gave me this basic framework of an ascending and a descending arrow. The ascent is humanity and the evolving world reaching up toward God in the introduction and chapter one, then the descent is God's reaching down to humans through revelation (ch.IV) and Jesus (ch.V). This image of two arrows aiming at each other can help the reader to discover the interconnection between chapters. Human and cosmic groping open the question of what is so special about Christianity (ch.II): personalism(ch.III) and Word of God(ch.IV). The rest of the book is about God reaching out to humanity's groping through revelation and Jesus.

The topics of the book are traditional and in hindsight they unintentionally mirror perspectives of the great Franciscan theologian Bonaventure. Bonaventure's greatest work is *The Soul's Journey into God*. In that work he arranges numerous pathways to God in terms of three pairs of wings which correspond to Francis of Assisi's vision of the sixth winged seraph superimposed upon Christ crucified. The lower pair of wings points to creation as a way to God. The middle pair points to the human person as a way of finding God and the upward pair of wings points to God Himself as Being and as Trinity. These focal point creation, human person, and God are congruent with *Christian Footings: C*reation, Personalism, and God through Jesus..

The sources in the anthology are Catholic. In addition to an important official document(from Vatican II), I purposely wanted the sources to be samples of some of the best writers in that tradition. Catholic is more than officialdom. The creative efforts of such people as Teilhard de Chardin and Thomas Merton were at times in conflict with the bureaucratic church; their work deserves exposure every bit as much as what comes down through the approved channels. Jesus was a religious critic, and his life is a testimony to the courage of those whose insights do as much to challenge institutions as to support them. My hope is readers will use the anthology as a stepping off point to sample the writing of great authors whose works await discovery.

Introduction

Critical historical study of the Bible and the theory of evolution were two of the greatest challenges to Christianity in the nineteenth century. Both perspectives focus on the dimension of time, and time threatened the security derived from an eternal and unchanging view of Christian doctrine.

The theory of evolution gave an explanation of the world that did not include God and appeared to be in conflict with the Genesis account of creation in six days. The teaching of evolution was banned in Tennessee public schools until 1968! Was Christian teaching out of date, irrelevant, or simply one story among others? Christian claims to be the exclusive possessor of ultimate truth were undermined by this theory.

The development of critical historical study similarly challenged Christian doctrine. The texts of the Bible though sacred to Christians, nevertheless came under the analytical scrutiny of historians and those who used critical historical methods. Conflicts between different versions of the same stories raised questions about truth and historical accuracy. Furthermore exposure to world literature unearthed parallels to biblical stories, such as the flood, that raised questions about the uniqueness of biblical accounts.

Broadly speaking Christian thinkers who embraced evolution and critical history are sometimes labeled as liberals; the Christian resistance to these nineteenth century movements of critical history and evolution is called fundamentalism.[1]

Fundamentalism is a term often uttered out of the side of the mouth or invoked when there is international trouble or national embarrassment. While general use of the term is negative, there are those who are proud to call themselves fundamentalists. Not only are usages positive and negative, but there are also Protestant, Catholic, Islamic, and Jewish fundamentalists. How can all of this diversity fit one term?

The most global usage, the one that reaches across religious boundaries as diverse as Christian, Islamic, and Jewish, applies to those religious people who are suspicious of the contemporary world, of communism, of modern morality, or modern fashions and music, and/or of contemporary sexual attitudes. These people are generally distrustful of and defensive toward secularization, a cultural shift away from God and religious values. Clearly Islamic, Christian, and Jewish fundamentalists are divided on many fronts, even in their distrust of modernity, and their respective condemnations differ. Nevertheless these true believers would agree about many of the dangerous trends in our world though an Iranian Islamic fundamentalist and an American Protestant fundamentalist might disagree about the specific length of hemlines.

This book takes the nineteenth century and twentieth century thought associated with critical history and evolution as part of the fabric of contemporary Christian thought. The assumption is that Christianity flourishes through alignment with science and history and the other disciplines that expand human understanding. Christianity will perish by association with evil, but these disciplines are not evil!

This assumption of the compatibility between Christianity and other disciplines expresses the belief in the basic goodness of human nature which is a foundation of this book's understanding of Christianity. Christianity embraced the Genesis account of creation in which God decreed the world to be "very good." Creatures reflect the Divine goodness; the internal world of human consciousness shares in both that goodness and in an orientation to become more like God.

Early Christianity saw this openness toward God in human beings in a variety of ways. In the second century, Clement of Alexandria, for example, recognized knowledge of God and morality in some of the Greek philosophers. Their ability to know truth is not dependent upon Christianity but upon the gift of reason.[2] He respected Plato because he recognizes the goal of human life as becoming more like God.[3] He saw human reason as a God given image of the perfect Image, Christ, and the *Logos*. He plays on the dual meanings of *logos* (word, reason):

> Heraclitus said well "men are gods and gods are men, for reason is the same" (Fragment 62)--manifestly a mystery. God is in man and a man is God, as the Mediator, fulfilling the will of His Father. For the reason common to both is the mediator; that is, the Word, Son of God, savior of man, the servant of God, our Educator.[4]

Human goodness is rooted in God's goodness as creator; God further endorses creation by sending Jesus to become part of creation.

Augustine, though often accused of being preoccupied with sin also stands with an acknowledgment of the goodness of nature through a built in restlessness for God. He opens the *Confessions* by addressing

God: ". . . you have made us for yourself, and our hearts are restless until they find rest in you."[5] Augustine follows beauty, truth, and goodness to discover that the beautiful bodies and captivating ideas he pursued were all reflections of God.

> Behold you were within, and I abroad, and there I searched for you. Deformed I, plunging amid those fair forms, which you have made. You were with me, but I was not with you. Things kept me far from you, which unless they were in you were not at all. You called and shouted and burst my deafness. You flashed, shouted and scattered my blindness. You breathed odors and I drew in breath and pant for you. I tasted and hunger and thirst. You touched me and I burned for your peace."[6]

Augustine's quest charts a path of the human soul toward God. It is no accident that both he and Clement were inspired by platonic writings. Plato in the *Symposium* and the *Phaedrus* speaks of the ascent and nourishment of the soul by beauty, wisdom, and goodness. These qualities are divine and are reflected however dimly in earthly realities. The soul when clear in understanding sees beautiful things, truth, and good things as pointers to a transcendent realm. Early and medieval Christianity took this framework as articulating the nature of God and the human soul.

Twentieth century writers such as Marechal, Rahner, and Lonergan tap into this early Christian and platonic tradition to say that the tendency within humans to go beyond their own grasp is a pointer toward God. Humans desire whatever is good, true and beautiful. Human experience is that desire leads to acquisition and temporary satisfaction. Eventually desire for some other good thing or a new question demanding another truth, leads onward. What is the direction and meaning of this restlessness, of this desiring that no limited truth or good thing can satisfy? Does the desire to know lead to an endless series? What is the point of human desire or intentionality? These writers along with W. N. Clarke would say that of course no finite truth or good thing can satisfy a human being completely as humans are made for Infinite Truth and Goodness. The unrestricted capacity to raise new questions and the restlessness of the human heart are traces of the image of God within them leading them toward sharing in God's life.[7]

NOTES

1. See Sydney E. Ahlstrom, *A Religious History of the American People* (New Haven: Yale University Press, 1972), 763-784.

---

2. Clement of Alexandria *Stromata* V.94.

3. *Stromata* II, 100.

4. Clement *Instructor* II, 2

5. Augustine *Confessions* I, 1.

6. *Confessions* X, 27.

7. See for example W. N. Clarke. "The Dynamism of the Spirit" in John Heaney, *Psyche and Spirit*. Rev.ed.(Paulist, 1984), 64-80.

I. Creation:
Pierre Teilhard de Chardin

A. Christianity and Evolution.

Movement and change are two of the most pervasive characteristics of contemporary experience. Everything seems to be in flux: values, beliefs, lifestyles, customs, and rituals. Nothing appears to be immune to the movement of reality. Movement and change are perennial elements, but we in the contemporary world have a sense of movement that our ancestors did not. For the people of the pre-modern world, creation is a static framework in which individuals change. Ignatius of Loyola in the sixteenth century, for example, writes in his *Spiritual Exercises* that people are to praise and serve God and to use creation in so far as creation aids in individual salvation. ("First Principle and Foundation") Creation is the dependable backdrop for individual transformation. What we cannot escape in the modern world is the awareness that creation is changing along with individual human beings. The change is not merely movement but transformation. The concept of evolution gives even the nonscientifically educated person a sense that the world today grew out of a series of yesterdays.

Christians of all flavors initially were caught off guard by the concept of evolution. Christianity did not come with a ready-made view of the universe. The Bible gives a series of pictures about God creating by speaking and by molding clay, and Christians concluded that everything owes existence to God. Up until the first half of the twentieth century most mainstream Christians took literally the pictures of the way the Bible presents God's creative activity. Further challenges to Christian imagination are the discoveries of the immensities of space and time.[1] The Biblical dimensions of space and time: several thousand years and the Mediterranean region and its surroundings are simply inadequate. With growing awareness of the prehistory of the earth and with knowledge of comparable creation stories in non-biblical literature, mainstream Christian churches have let go of the literal interpretation of the first few chapters of the Bible. They maintain that reality comes from God, but now are willing to listen to science about how reality proceeds over a multi-billion year time span.

The Christian thinker who most helped the churches to integrate evolutionary ideas into Christian thought is Pierre Teilhard de Chardin ("Teilhard" for short). Teilhard's bridge building between science and Christianity emerged from his life-long dual-pronged romance. The great loves of his life were God and the earth, and he was unwilling to turn away from either for the other. As a child Teilhard used to collect stones and found a fascination in their durability. Rock hardness gave him a sense of permanence. One day he added to his stones an iron bolt; when he returned to his little drawer to inspect his iron bolt, he was shocked to see that this extremely hard substance was decaying through rust. For permanence Teilhard looked to and through the earth, not away from it, to God.

Teilhard developed his two loves by studying the earth and becoming a paleontologist and by serving God through the Society of Jesus as a priest. Born in 1881 in France, the year before the death of Charles Darwin, Teilhard became a Jesuit in 1902. In the early 1920's while Americans were fascinated by the legal questions raised by the Scopes Monkey trial over the appropriateness of teaching evolution in the public schools, Teilhard was writing about original sin in an evolutionary context. Roman censors did not welcome Teilhard's opinions about original sin, and he was pressured into signing a statement of belief in the stories of Genesis as literally true. Teilhard's submission expressed his willingness to wait for Church bureaucrats to catch up and enter the twentieth century. He in no way retreated from his vision of an evolving world where Christ was nevertheless central. Teilhard pursued his paleontological research in China where he was safe from western fear about evolution. In China he had the time to continue to sketch his Christian vision, but he was in a kind of exile. He remained unheralded by his own Christian community for the rest of his life. Due to Christian misunderstanding, Teilhard did not live to see the publication of his masterwork, *The Phenomenon of Man*. He died in New York on Easter Sunday, 1955, relatively unknown.

Teilhard creatively stretched the understanding of Christians at a time when they were largely either defensive or confused about Christianity and science. At the same time Teilhard attempted to offer the scientifically minded a vision of reality more personal than the confines of empirical science would allow.

Teilhard read the world through the eyes of a paleontologist, and what he saw was convergence. He also read the world through Christian eyes and saw the cosmic scope of personalization.

B. To See or Perish

Teilhard studied the past in order to understand the direction of the future. As he read the pre-history of the earth, he saw patterns of continuity and growth, not random disorder. The pattern operating within the earth process, Teilhard called the law of complexity consciousness. What this means is that through time greater complexity and consciousness have emerged on the face of the earth. By greater complexity Teilhard means an increase in complexity of form and organization. A carbon atom is simpler than an amoeba; an amoeba is simpler than a chicken; a human being is more complex than a chicken. From atom to molecule to inorganic molecule to cell to multi-celled organisms to vertebrates to mammals to primates to humans, there is an increase in complexity. That increase in complexity, Teilhard asserts, has evolved through time.

Increase of complexity carries with it a corresponding increase in consciousness. To understand this, one needs to mention another of Teilhard's concepts, "the within." The within is the inner face of reality. Teilhard believed that all reality had an inner dimension; by inner he means a component or dimension that is not directly observable. If not directly observable, it nevertheless can be approached by reason. What is the difference between a tree and a log? The matter of a tree is not different from that of the log it becomes. What is the difference? The tree is holding together as a unity, but the log is decomposing into lesser unities. The within of the tree has been lost. The within is that which holds a thing together as a unity. The log is composed of organic molecules; whatever holds molecules together as unities are the withins of the molecules. This interior principle is called "interior" because it is not directly seen.

Higher consciousness characterizes higher levels of reality and later developments in the evolutionary process. Thus humans have higher consciousness than chickens, and chickens have higher consciousness than trees. If consciousness is not observable, how do we know which beings have higher consciousness than others? Teilhard focuses on behavior as the clue to consciousness, and the particular behavior he selects is spontaneity. Dogs are more spontaneous than earthworms; dogs play. Dogs are less tied to instinct than worms. If we placed an earthworm on a table and tried to predict its behaviors in an hour, we would have a fairly short list of activities. If we tried to predict what a dog would do in an hour, we would have a longer list. If we were to try to predict what a small boy would do in an hour, we would need a computer. Spontaneity admits of degrees, and the higher degree reflects higher degrees of consciousness. (The connection of all of this with spirituality will become clear shortly.)

At the moment we see that according to Teilhard the evolutionary process has led to a gradual increase in consciousness; spirituality will more obviously be on center stage when humans ask about the direction of the future and recognize their own responsibility for the future. We need to give greater foundation to any such questioning if spirituality is to be well rooted in the earth process.

Teilhard addressed both scientists and Christians. When scientists look at the earth process, among what they see are the two laws of thermodynamics. The first law states that matter/energy are a constant amount on the earth; matter/energy cannot be created nor destroyed but can be transformed. The second law is the troublesome one; it is contained in the term "entropy." This law states that there is a tendency toward the dissipation of energy, that is, through time less and less energy is available for doing work. Work, as Barry Commoner has commented "is what doesn't get done unless you do it." Though the amount of energy does not change in the universe, the amount available for serving human needs is diminishing. That is one of the reasons why we have energy crises. If on a cold day you open the window, there is a tendency for the heat to go out the window. The likelihood that heat will turn around and re-enter the window is extremely small; re-entry is not going to happen! The heat going out the window is a function of entropy. In order to replace that heat, some work needs to be done in the boiler room. The available energy for doing work diminishes through time; that is part of the sad story science tells.

This law of entropy is true, but it does not have the last word in Teilhard's view. If entropy had the last word, the earth and its inhabitants would be doomed to a bleak future. We are running out of steam; we are going downhill. Teilhard is acutely aware that if people believe that they are headed for a dead end, they will not walk in that direction. They will certainly not give their best creative efforts to a dead end. If the earth process is heading for a blind alley, how will humanity rise to the challenges of the future?

Teilhard's answer is "to see or perish." Unless people can see a positive outcome for humanity, they will not relate in a positive and constructive way to the earth. Here he reminds those who despair before the specter of entropy that entropy deals only with the outer face of reality. The inner face of reality, as we have seen above, reveals that there has been an increase in consciousness. The obvious pinnacle of that process is human consciousness.

Teilhard distinguishes human consciousness from lower levels of awareness by the activity of reflection. Reflection involves the human ability to transcend an immediate experience by creating mental distance. If I feel cold, my entire awareness is not taken up with coldness; I can step out of my experience and think about my situation of being cold and how to change my situation. If a lower animal feels cold, it is more limited in the changes it can perform on its situation. A cold dog can sit on another dog or on some leaves, or eat more food. Humans have created houses, insulation, clothing, heating systems, coffee makers, and portable hand warmers out of the distance that reflection provides.

Humans are able to reflect upon the process of evolution itself. We stand in the present and survey the past, and on the basis of the direction of the process of evolution can estimate the direction of the future. If people see only entropy, the future will not stimulate the best of human motivation; if they see the rise in consciousness, Teilhard believes people have a better chance of meeting the challenges ahead.

When Teilhard stands on the peak of the present, what does he see? He sees a time of increased moral burden. The possibility of world destruction is greater than ever. Since the twentieth century we can now end human life. The future depends on human choice; we cannot expect there to be a natural unfolding of the future unless humans make the right choices. In other words for there to be a future, the evolutionary process must pass through human consciousness. The human being is evolution conscious of itself. We are part of the process and also hold the tiller, at least of humanity's future, in our hands.

Destruction is not the inevitable choice; Teilhard sees some unifying elements shaping themselves in the world. There is first of all the geographical curvature of the earth. As population increases people are confined to the surface of the earth, and the population compresses. If fifteen people sat in an average sized classroom, students would not be especially aware of each other. If another fifty students were added to the room, each would become aware of the persons on either side or at least of the elbows of their neighbors. Such is the force of compression that results from the increase of population over the geographical curvature of the earth.

Teilhard writes of another force of compression, namely the mental curvature of the earth. By this he means that when a new idea surfaces in one part of the earth the rest of the earth, as it is similarly prepared, will soon receive that new idea. Satellite dishes for televisions in rural America were quickly accepted in Mexico and other developing nations. They already had television sets; the satellite dish was a small step.

If there are such forces of compression, are there not grounds for optimism? The geographical curvature of the earth is forcing people to think about one another, and the mental curvature is enabling new ideas to be communicated globally. We have to admit that in our century there has been a mutation in consciousness toward global awareness. Generally we know more about what is happening around the world than our ancestors knew. Is not world unity a likely development? It is a necessity, but we can fail to choose unity.

Failure is easy to imagine. Think of shrinking resources coupled with human greed. In a small city in Kansas where I used to live, a Woolco discount store was going out of business. Each week a sign would go up advertising 20% off of the prices of all merchandise, then 30%, then 40% off. Finally, as one of my students reported who was in Woolco on its last night, a voice announced to all shoppers that they could have whatever they could grab in the next 10 minutes for $25. You can imagine the chaotic shoving and leaping, not a place for the elderly or the infirm. I can easily picture a time on earth when the forces of compression could transform human society to the last night at Woolco.

Teilhard admits that the forces of compression alone will not lead to world unity and peace. At best they set the stage for possible unity, but forces of compression are coercive. People will not be forced into giving the best they have to give. The motivation to give of oneself requires freedom, and Teilhard believes love is the necessary ingredient.

How can egoism be overcome? How are humans going to pull together to build the earth and to meet the increasing moral challenges of the future? What can evoke the motivation to love in an unselfish way? Will capitalism or Marxism stir the depths of human love? Teilhard thinks not, because these are only ideas, and ideas receive and appreciate nothing. If one loves a dog, it can appreciate affection, but how could it appreciate what it means for a human to love? Other humans

can receive the depths of human self giving, but even other human beings do not know all that is in another's heart. Christian tradition would
say only God can fully receive and appreciate all that a human has to
give. Thus Teilhard believes that the attractive power of God is the
necessary source of motivation that can overcome human egoism and
lead to a more unified and peaceful human society. Without personal
love, without super-personal love, people may not bring their best energies to the earth process.

Teilhard believes people will make the right choices; he does not
think we will manage to thwart several billion years of evolution. The
path of survival, however, will involve cooperating with God. This is
not to say that Teilhard believed everyone needs to believe in God, but
that awareness of God would help.

C. Christ/God: Evolver and Omega

God for Teilhard is the one who is drawing consciousness to higher
levels and leading humanity to seek social unity. The name Teilhard
uses for God is Omega, the last letter of the Greek alphabet that the
New Testament applies to Christ. God as the end of evolutionary striving explains the driving force of evolution. John's Gospel gives us a
text to show the Christian logic of Teilhard's understanding: "No one
can come to me unless the Father . . . draws him."(John 6:44) In light
of this, who but God could be responsible for drawing the earth process
to the point where it (in humans) can relate consciously to God? Thus
God by attraction is working on the human mass.

The way God is active on earth is primarily through love. Teilhard
defines love as "the affinity of being with being."[2] The tendency for
beings to unite is love. On the human level that uniting must pass
through reflection and moral freedom, but not so in the subhuman
foundations of love. Below the human level, love is the power of attraction and unification. Thus when atoms unite to form molecules, or
when cells form organisms the power of love (also conceived of as
God's drawing power) is at work. The unification that is present in the
earth is evidence of God's work, and now in humans God has given the
possibility of relating in a conscious and free way to Himself and to His
plan for the world.

In addition to describing God as the driving force of evolution, Teilhard relates God to the future in a way that promotes human commitment to the earth rather than escape from the earth. The problem of
living in time is one of the perennial religious issues. All human aspi-

rations, thoughts, images, ideas arise and are blown into the past like so many autumn leaves. What is a person to make of aging, decay, and deterioration? How can a person deal with loss of time, never to be retrieved? The sense of loss associated with passing time may make the ascending arrow of the human spirit wobble with doubt; the great loss of death can bend that arrow back upon itself into the form of a question mark.

With his commitment to evolution, Teilhard looks to the future to answer this question of human temporality, yet he is critical of any idea of progress which does not face squarely the question of death or the question a person is in the face of death. Teilhard feels the sting of temporality in the need for meaning: "without the assurance that this tomorrow exists, can we really go on living."[3] Teilhard is not content with traditional answers to the problem of living in time. One of those answers involves turning away from time and turning toward the eternal in oneself. This detachment from whatever is time bound, from whatever is transient is a component of spiritualities both eastern and western. Whatever the wisdom of such turning away, commitment to the earth (which God so loves) is neglected. A more classically Christian approach to the problem of human temporality is to encourage people to find God in the present moment. The Eternal has embraced the temporal in creation and in the Incarnation. To find God in the present moment is important if one is not to use the future as an escape from an unfulfilled present, but here again the earth process is likely to be overlooked. This first step of finding God in the here and now is God Above, God above time. Teilhard affirms this notion of God but adds that God as Omega is in the future. God is Ahead as well as Above.

God is drawing human energy, commitment, and love toward a more unified social reality. Teilhard states this with characteristic inspiration:

> Once things are seen in this light, it is impossible to adhere to Christ without doing all one can to assist the whole forward drive. In that same light, too communion becomes an impassioned participation in universal action; and expectation of the parousia merges exactly...with the coming of a maturity of man; and the upward movement towards the "above" combines harmoniously with the drive "ahead"...And from all this follows that Christian charity, generally presented as a mere soothing lotion poured over the world's suffering, is seen to be the most complete and most active agent of hominization.[4]

The unity toward which God is leading, Teilhard finds in the New Testament, mainly in Pauline literature. Paul speaks of God (or Christ) becoming all in all. (1 Cor. 15:28) He also writes of all things being made for God. (Col 1:16)   How is everything to be filled with God, and how are all things to be given over to God except through humanity? As more humans yield to God and commit themselves to God's work of unification, He will become all in all. This increase in God's influence over the population of the earth, Teilhard calls Christogenesis. This means the coming into being of Christ. As Christ extends his influence over more people the evolutionary process will continue to unfold in harmony with his plan. Christ is God Omega, a notion which includes the unification in love of the people of the earth. When the potential for love is realized in humanity, that will be the second coming of Christ.

The second coming of Christ for Teilhard is to be found within humanity as the body of Christ. This picture is in contrast to Paul's picture in First Thessalonians of Christ coming on the clouds (no telescopes in Paul's day). If Christ is coming on the clouds, the posture of Christians is to wait. God will do what needs to be done. In Teilhard's understanding Christ is coming through human faith, hope, love, and action. Christ's coming depends on humanity's cooperation, and humanity's work needs to be applied to building the earth not just waiting for a heavenly appearance. Thus Teilhard's notions of God and Christ include commitment to history and the earth process, a vision of Christian life that is more active than in ages past. Some who expect apocalyptic cosmic upheaval will find Teilhard's vision too rosy. For the biblically minded among them I would ask, "After the cosmic upheavals pictured in the Bible, is God going to be all in all or not?"

Teilhard gives some alternative images for the future and for the end of history, but his images keep Christ in the center. Teilhard's vision gives new life to a fertile but fairly uncultivated symbol, Omega. For Teilhard, Omega is a name both for the cosmic Christ who is drawing creation to Himself and for the culmination of the process as the population of the earth unifies in God.

Teilhard calls Christians to find God through commitment to their earthly involvements rather than through an exclusively otherworldly spirituality that is disconnected from creation. He insists that Christian activity finds its value in more than the pure intention to serve God. The intention to serve God needs to be linked to one's understanding of what God is trying to accomplish in the earth process.

Teilhard further offers Christians and opportunity to resist the temptation to tie Christianity to a view of the cosmos that is at odds with mainstream education: no need for separate creationism science, no need for a split between one's scientific education and one's view of the world as a Christian. Teilhard does not believe everyone will become Christian, but his vision encourages Christians to join hands with any who are truly building the earth.

D. Historical resonance

Teilhard's understanding of Christianity is geared to the contemporary world, yet his influence within Christianity draws strength from Christian history. His understanding of Christ as cosmic finds historical footing in the Pauline understanding of the Cosmic Christ (especially in Ephesians, Colossians, and to a lesser extent in 1 Corinthians) and in the Word of God in the prologue to John's Gospel. These New Testament writers showed Jesus to be the incarnation of the earlier Jewish notion of wisdom personified who was God's master craftsman in creation (as in Proverbs 8). After the New Testament linkage of Jesus with God's original creative activity prior to the Incarnation, writers after the New Testament period saw Jesus as God's *Logos* or God's reason or self-expression.

Clement of Alexandria (150?- 215?), for example, saw Christ as the *Logos* (reason, mind) of God and saw creation as containing God's wisdom for any who had eyes to see. In this way Clement explained to himself how non-Christian philosophers were capable of learning truth about God and morality apart from the Bible. Clement believed the Bible to be a more readable and trustworthy source of Divine teaching, but creation was not unintelligible.

Creation for Clement, and for numerous other writers in the early Christian centuries, was marked by God its author. If one is familiar with Vivaldi, one will recognize that a work is by Vivaldi even if one has never heard that particular work before. In this way Clement and Christians like him believed Christ (as Divine Wisdom) could be found in creation. Furthermore people imaged God's Reason (*Logos*, Christ) by being equipped with reason themselves. As God could generate ideas, so can human beings. Humans marked by sin have to work hard to listen to Teacher guidance from within and teachers from without through creation and the Scriptures. Christian spirituality largely consists in following the Instructor God sent.

More than living according to the dictates of the Divine Teacher, Christian life developed into a vision of God through creation. God could be glimpsed indirectly through his manifestations. Whether the symmetry of a tiger's face or the head of a cabbage or the grandeur of a sunset, these created objects can trigger intuitions of God's creative presence.

In the Middle Ages, Francis of Assisi and Bonaventure are the prominent mystic and theologian of creation respectively. Both of their horizons are sensitive to creation, yet their creation centered gaze remained Christ centered. From the joy producing manifestations of God in creation, both Francis and Bonaventure rose to their Divine source, Christ the Mediator of creation.

E. Critique

Teilhard continues and extends the creation centered approach to life and Christ. He casts the Christian mysteries into a cosmos marked by an ascent through time called evolution. As Christians become more comfortable with evolution they will find in Teilhard a door to traditional Christian sources as well as a window to the ecologically enlightened future.

Teilhard is a visionary, and his vision is not a matter of technique. If there are any how-to recommendations, I would say that the approach of Teilhard is a matter of awareness. To cultivate his awareness of the direction of creation, reading his books would be the best step to take.

Beyond reading, the challenge he holds out to people is to search for the link between their own activity and the vision of the future that Teilhard paints. To recognize that link is to open to the possibility of adoration through the simplest of tasks.

Teilhard's thought continues to inspire such an earth-conscious author such as Thomas Berry. Their thought along with lively developments in ecologically aware theology can help Christians to integrate the earth in their Christian commitments.

Berry's critique of Teilhard can help Teilhard's thought to live in an earth-sensitive Christianity. Berry believes that Teilhard is not sufficiently concerned with the destruction of the earth wrought by industrial society. He sees Teilhard as heir to the "imperial tradition in human-earth relations, the tradition of human control over the natural world."[5] Teilhard writes: "When mankind has once realized that its first function is to penetrate intellectually unify, and harness the energies which surround it, in order still further to understand and master them, there will no longer be any danger of running into an upper limit of its florescence."[6] Thus Teilhard supports the goals of industrial society.

Teilhard's thought is so important in that it is "so comprehensive in its overarching perspectives" that it should not be lost but rather adjusted. Furthermore Teilhard's context can protect the ecological movement from "trivialization." [7](Berry, p.22) The key principle that Teilhard lacks is the principle of "a total earth community...the earth itself and all its living and non-living components is a community, that the human is a member of this integral community and finds its proper role in advancing the well-being of this community." (p.21) The norm for evaluating persons, institutions, and activities is "the extent to which they foster or obstruct the creative functioning of the larger earth community, the community of all those components that constitute the planet." (p.21)

Berry believes Teilhard needs to be adapted to the insights of the later decades of the twentieth century.

1. Evolution needs to be inclusive: "the evolutionary process finds its highest expression in the earth community seen in its comprehensive dimensions, not simply in a human community reigning in triumphal domination over the other components of the earth community...Human convergence at the expense of planetary convergence is inherently destructive for both the human community and the planetary community. There can be only one final destiny for the entire community." (p.23)

2. Consciousness: "The proper role of human intelligence would be not to exploit but to enhance the natural world and its functioning. The basic norm would be, not the human, but the well-being and integral functioning of the earth community." (p.26)   3. The sacred: Teilhard's affirmation of creation needs to include articulation of an acceptable relationship between the human and the earth. The complex systems of the biosphere need protection from human destructiveness; human striving for spiritual consciousness cannot justify biocide.

4. Activation of energy: those who would continue Teilhard's thought need to increase appreciation of how the natural world continues to support human physical and psychological life. The human imagination and range of emotional sensitivity as well as the sense of the sacred are all nourished by the natural world.

5. Science: Whatever the benefits of "earlier engineering projects, they have led to a planetary devastation beyond measuring." (p. 30) Science and future technologies need to be judged by "the well-being of the earth community in the full extent and variety of its manifestations." (p.31)

Berry's critique of Teilhard helps to free Teilhard from some of the blindness of the industrial age. With Teilhard's foundation and Berry's adjustment, Christianity can look toward the future with feet planted in the earth and develop a Christian vision that is simultaneously in tune with science, the gospel, and the ecological age.

F. Resources

Primary

Teilhard de Chardin, Pierre. *Christianity and Evolution.* N.Y.: Harcourt, Brace, Jovanovich, 1969.
———. *The Divine Milieu* . N.Y.: Harper & Row, 1969.
———. *The Future of Man.* N.Y.: Harper & Row, 1964.
———. *The Phenomenon of Man* . N.Y.: Harper & Row, 1965.
———. *Toward the Future* . N.Y.: Harcourt, Brace, Jovanovich, 1975.

Secondary

Berry, Thomas. *Dream of the Earth* . S.F.: Sierra Club Books, 1990.
———. *Teilhard in the Ecological Age.* Chambersburg, Pa.: Anima Books, 1982.
———. *The Universe Story.* N.Y.: Harper San Francisco, 1992.
Haught, John. *Science and Religion: From Conflict to Conversation.* N.Y.: Paulist Press, 1995.
Johnson, Elizabeth "Does God Play Dice? Divine Providence and Chance" *Theological Studies* 57(1996): 3-18.
McDaniel, Jay. *Of God and Pelicans* . Louisville: Westminster, 1989.
Maloney, George. *The Cosmic Christ.* N. Y.: Sheed & Ward, 1969.
Schmitz-Moormann, Karl. *Theology of Creation in an Evolutionary World.* Cleveland: Pilgrim, 1997

NOTES

1. See Charles Taylor's *A Secular Age* (Harvard, 2007), chapter 9 for excellent discussion on the changed sense of the world in recent centuries.

2. Pierre Teilhard de Chardin, *The Phenomenon of Man* (N.Y.: Harper &Row,1965), 264.

3. 228.

4. Teilhard, *Toward the Future* (N.Y.: Harcourt, Brace, Jovanovich, 1975), 204.

5. Thomas Berry, *Teilhard in the Ecological Age* (Chambersburg, Pa.: Anima Books, 1982), 16.

6. *Phenomenon of Man*, 280, quoted in Berry, 17.

7. Berry, 22.

II. Christianity and World Religions

A. Situation: Global Consciousness

With no special individual effort, people are born into global consciousness. We have an awareness of events in China, Europe, Latin America, and Israel largely thanks to radio and television. Imagine the awareness of American pioneers heading westward from the eastern states. For all but a few, they would have remembered their home towns and port cities. Even these memories would be dimming without frequent fresh supplies of images and messages that we currently expect.

In addition to a growing awareness of events throughout the world, increased mobility and education mean that people of different cultures are interacting to a high degree. How does Christianity fit into this world situation where it is one of many options?

Christianity has a long tradition of exclusivism. The idea that Christianity is the true religion and others are either imperfect expressions of truth or simply false paths has roots in the sacred texts of Christianity. From the Hebrew Bible Christians learn of the Jews as God's chosen people. The New Testament replaces the 12 tribes of Israel with the 12 apostles; Moses is replaced by Jesus; the old son of God (Israel) is replaced by the new son of God (Jesus). In other words early Christians played one-upmanship with some of the most precious symbols of Judaism. One of the consequences of this effort of Christians to portray Christianity as the fulfillment of Jewish expectation is the enduring mentality of being chosen by God. Throughout Christian history an attitude dominant among Christians has been that Jesus has been chosen by God as the way of salvation for humankind and that Christians have been chosen to promote the knowledge and love of Jesus. Christianity has seen itself since New Testament days to be a world-wide missionary movement: "Go therefore and make disciples of all nations, baptizing them in the name of the Father, Son, and Holy Spirit." (Matthew 28) The New Testament also contains absolute statements that belief in Jesus and baptism are necessary for salvation. "No one can enter the kingdom of God without being born of water and spirit...Whoever believes in him will not be condemned, but whoever does not believe has already been condemned, because he has not believed in the name of the only Son of God." (John 3) As contemporary Christians interact with good people of other religious traditions or of no religious tradition they increasingly do not share the exclusivism of earlier generations. This gradual move away from Christian tribalism does not mean that many Christians still believe that belief in Jesus is not necessary for salvation. Aside from Christian fundamentalists, the eminent Reformed theologian Karl Barth thought that non-Christians were in a state of peril and needed the help of the Christian sources in order to find their way to God. Still the mainstream is moving away from exclusivism as represented by the Second Vatican Council.

B. Inclusivism and Beyond to Pluralism

In the series of meetings of Catholic bishops in the mid-1960s called Vatican II a number of important statements were made concerning the relationship between Christianity and world religions. An entire document is titled "Declaration on the Relationship of the Church to Non-Christian Religions,"(most of this document is included in the Anthology section of this book). This document mentions various religions by name with a brief description and then affirms their validity. "The Catholic Church rejects nothing which is true and holy in these religions. She looks with sincere respect upon those ways of conduct and of life, those rules and teachings which, though differing in many particulars from what she hold and sets forth, nevertheless often reflect a ray of that Truth which enlightens all men. Indeed, she proclaims and must ever proclaim Christ, 'the way, the truth, and the life' (John 14:6) in whom men find the fullness of religious life..."[1] Other religions contain elements of truth and holiness, hence the grace of God and Christ are present in those religions. This document nevertheless affirms that Christ is normative: "the way." Most of what Vatican II says about the relationship between Christianity and world religions shows respect to other traditions and sees them as fulfilled in Christianity. This position is variously called theology of fulfillment or inclusivism, meaning that other religions are included in God's activity.

While affirming what is beneficial to humanity in other religions, Vatican II believes that Christianity may be of service to world religions. Suppose for example one encounters the kind of horror story that missionaries tell such as the sacrifice of a human being in order to secure the favor of some god. In such a case, Christianity's teaching about the dignity of the human person and persons as images of God would serve to correct the religious belief of those people who would sacrifice human being out of fear of divine wrath or of evil spirits.

While affirming what is good and holy in other religions and continuing to see Christianity as the clearest expression of God's revelation, Vatican II takes a step beyond exclusivism. Vatican II suggests that Christians could learn from other traditions. Vatican II counsels Christian missionaries "to assimilate the ascetic and contemplative traditions whose seeds were sometimes already planted by God in ancient cultures prior to the preaching of the gospel."[2] The context of this learning of the contemplative traditions of other traditions is to foster the reception of Christ among non-Christians through adaptation to their cultures. Thus rather than learning something from these cultures for the sake of spiritual benefit of Christians, the learning is to facilitate communication with those who will eventually benefit from accepting Christ.

This position of accepting that the grace of God is found beyond the confines of Christianity is certainly a posture more respectful of non-Christians than Christian exclusivism. Yet how can Christians justify acknowledging the presence of Christ beyond Christianity? Most simply Christian theology since the New Testament has seen Christ to be the word and wisdom of God. (John 1) All of God's creative activity includes Christ as word and wisdom. This type of reflection on biblical sources may be helpful for Christians, but since only Christians and Jews pay much attention to the Bible, a more theologically philosophical approach may yield a broader base for dialog with non-biblical peoples.

The theologian who has the most developed explanation of this position is Karl Rahner. Rahner has a theologically anthropological starting point. He observes that humans have a natural openness to God. This natural openness manifests itself through human restlessness. When humans want to understand something, they raise questions and answer them. Answers only temporarily satisfy the desire to know. People will raise new questions and that process of raising new questions involves going beyond whatever finite knowledge one has acquired. This going beyond the finite is the human way of pointing beyond the finite toward the infinite. The same process occurs in the desire for good things. The person yearns for something and after acquiring that good thing, the desire for another good thing arises. This going beyond good things is another pointer toward the infinite. Rahner has a more complicated way of talking about the natural openness to the Infinite or God, but the important point is to see this tendency to transcend the limited that is part of human experience. This pointing to God, Rahner calls the transcendental presence of God.   God is present in human hearts, and that is why humans are never totally satisfied with the finite. Humans are reaching out toward God whether they know the word "God" or not.

This openness to God which is independent of the word "God": is called implicit faith by Rahner. Ideally with the proper circumstances people will seek to label the end of their yearning. The openness to God that humans experience is actually the subjective pole of God's tugging on the human heart and mind. God draws people to Himself through human desire for truth and goodness. (Augustine, Dionysius the Areopagite and other Platonically influenced Christian writers realized this many centuries before Rahner.) To surrender to the pull or call of God toward truth or goodness is to surrender to God. Thus when one is faced with a moral decision, and one knows what is right and surrenders to what one judges to be the right course, that surrender is an act of worship. To make an absolute moral decision despite the costs to one's pleasure or status is to surrender to God. To clarify further, the extreme situation of laying down one's life for one's friend, implies the reality of something beyond the self. That type of self-surrender is implicit faith. Rahner sees the proper labeling of the openness to God as explicit faith, and he sees the most correct conceptualization of God's presence as Christian faith. He also believes that the power of God seeks to express itself in human and fleshly terms inasmuch as God became human in Jesus. This enfleshing of the interior presence of God will be actualized in church life in ideal circumstances. Thus Rahner gives conceptual explanation of the idea that people can be living according to God even if they do not have the language about God. He calls such people anonymous Christians or anonymous theists(see the Anthology for a sample of Rahner's writing on this topic). Rahner gives a view of faith that is anthropologically based and can be affirmed by non-Christians. At the same time, however, he maintains the idea that Christianity fulfills non-Christian yearning. Non-Christians are likely to feel insulted if called anonymous Christians as though whatever is true and holy belongs to Christianity. Rahner's notion of anonymous Christian is helpful only to those Christians who need to justify the salvation of non-Christians.[3]

To move beyond the perspective that Christianity fulfills non-Christians, let us look to Raimundo Panikkar as an example of pluralism. Panikkar's interest in inter-religious dialog is more than academic. His first name is Spanish, and thanks to his Spanish mother, he is Catholic. His last name comes from his Hindu father. Panikkar focuses more on experience than dogma as he explores the relationship between Christianity and world religions. He uses both a Trinitarian model and a Hindu model from the *Bhagavad Gita* for exploring these relationships.

In *The Trinity and the Religious Experience of Man*, Panikkar uses the framework of the *Bhagavad Gita* to identify three types of spiritualities or religious styles. The *Gita* identifies the way of action, the way of love and the way of knowledge or wisdom.

The first of these ways Panikkar calls "iconolatry" which is the way of worship through images. What Panikkar means is relating to God with super-human characteristics. Thus God is a king, and people are expected to obey. Obedience to God may be expressed through careful observance of ritual.

The ritual action of this type of spirituality expresses adoration of God. The worshiper abandons and surrenders self to the image he or she has of God. Such ritual action, and the surrender it expresses can be found in a variety of religions including Hinduism, Islam, Christianity and Judaism.

The second type of spirituality is the way of love. As Bernard of Clairvaux said in the 12th century, God does not so much want reverence (which is iconolatry) as love. The way of love Panikkar calls personalism because it involves the cultivation of interpersonal love with God. Mutuality is the expression of inter-personal love. Obedience is still possible among lovers, but it is not the obedience of downcast eyes. This type of religious style which cultivates devotional love is strongly developed in Christianity and Hinduism.

The third type of spirituality is the way of knowledge, and the particular type of knowledge Panikkar means is the knowledge that the manifest (God as expressed) is one with the unmanifest (God as unexpressed). In other words, the way of knowledge is the way of nondualism where the person sees that God as unmanifest and the manifestations of God are not separate. God and the soul are not two, neither are they completely the same. The individual soul does not exhaust the Divine reality, yet is not separate either. Here God is not other; God is pure immanence. God is the unseen seer who sees through your own eyes, and acts through your hands. God is the center of your center. This non-dual experience is well developed in Hinduism and Buddhism; Christianity is not the best place to find this type of experience, though there have been some Christians who speak of this.

Here are three spiritual styles, and each may be associated with different religious traditions. Each religious tradition has a particular genius, and those traditions are especially valuable resources for spirituality. Thus if one is interested in personal love of God, Christianity or parts of Hinduism are the places to go. If one is interested in nondualism, try Hinduism or Buddhism.

Panikkar also uses a more Christian framework for understanding spiritual options. When Panikkar applies the Trinitarian model to religious experience, he associates each person of the Trinity with particular types of experience and with different religious traditions.

The Father is the mystery of God which is symbolized by silence. The mind and lips are silent before the Absolute One who is not to be reduced to human categories. Those people who are so aware of the immensity of God and the narrowness of their own minds worship God through silence. The refusal to pull God down to human terms is a form of reverence. This type of silence can be found in Buddhism; it is also present in apophatic traditions of Christianity, Judaism, and Islam.

Out of the silence of the Father proceeds the Word. God manifests as Word. Traditions that talk about God are the prophetic religions of Islam, Christianity, and Judaism. These religions say they have received messages from God for humanity. Where Buddhists do not talk about God, Christians feel duty-bound to do so. Christians have libraries dedicated to talking about God. The Christian missionary movement makes sense in this light as theirs is a religion of the Word that needs to be communicated. If one wants to learn about God, do not ask a Buddhist; ask a Christian or a Jew or a Moslem.

Out of the silence of the Father proceeds the Word, and the Word leads to Understanding. The Understanding that the Word offers is that the Father and the Word are one. Is this not the New Testament understanding of the function of the Holy Spirit, to enlighten people that the Son is one with the Father? The understanding that the Holy Spirit gives and here represents is nondualism. The immanence of God is the Holy Spirit. Again nondualism is highly developed in Hinduism.

What this Trinitarian model accomplishes, like the Hindu model above, is an identification of particular religious experiences with various religious traditions. No one religious tradition has a monopoly over these types of experiences, yet some traditions have developed these paths to a greater extent than others. This approach to inter-religious dialog does not totally relativize the particular genius of each tradition and avoids saying that all religions are talking about the same thing. This model does not claim that any particular experience or tradition is better than another. Its weakness may be its lack of a normative view of religion, yet each tradition tries to identify practices and beliefs that promote and also those that are contrary to human development.

C. Christ as Image of God

Panikkar's approach can help Christianity to dialog with other traditions with an openness to learn as well as teach. Furthermore, Christianity can use the above analysis to identify its own specialties, namely Word and Person. Christianity is a religion of revelation, of the Word of God. Furthermore, what is revealed is the personal love of God.

Christian exclusivists see Jesus Christ as the only savior. Vatican II and Rahner see Jesus as the fulfillment of human longing. Panikkar sees the Christ as the Lord that Christians call Jesus and "that other religious traditions call by a variety of names."[4] Panikkar's ambiguity about the uniqueness of Christ would not be satisfying to exclusivists or to Christian fulfillment theologians, but what he says that is positive about the Christ would be widely accepted. His focus is on spirituality and on description, not on doctrinal clarity.

The way Panikkar sees Christ ("Son") for a Christian is a mediator between divinity and humanity. The Christ is the expression of the unseen God, the icon of the Absolute, "the unique link between the created and the uncreated, the relative and absolute, the temporal and the eternal, earth and heaven." (p.53.)

All of these ideas are traditional and widely accepted. Where Panikkar departs from mainstream Christianity is in his assertion that the Christ is not identical with Jesus. "When I call this link between the finite and the infinite by the name Christ I am not presupposing its identification with Jesus of Nazareth." (p.53.) Where most Christians assume that Jesus is the Christ and the Christ is Jesus, Panikkar sees Christ as the universal and Jesus as the particular manifestation of the Christ.

Traditional Christianity sees the Father expressed through the Son and the Son expressed through Jesus. Panikkar sees the Father expressed through the Son and the Son expressed through Jesus and others.

The Christ of Panikkar would be the Lord as Christians know Him. Such a view of Christ fits nicely into a Hindu mentality and may facili-

tate inter-religious dialog. Such a view fits a Christ who reveals the
Father and a Christ who redeems by good example. This understanding
of Christ conflicts with some traditional formulations such as the
"only" begotten son of the Father, but biblical language about Jesus
expresses the enthusiasm of believers as much as timeless universal
doctrines.[5] In addition, to say that others are Lord, not merely Jesus,
might undermine the doctrine that says that the death and resurrection
of Christ atones for the sins of humankind.

The important question seems to be whether the non-affirmation of
the superiority and monopoly of Christ and Christianity would undermine the faith commitment of Christians. Hindus have lived for centuries with this type of awareness of a variety of incarnations. Roman
Catholics in the past few decades have become accustomed to the idea
that God is not confined to Christianity. Panikkar's view can remind
Christians that they do not possess exclusive and absolute truth.   The
knowledge of the Lord that Christianity offers is good for Christians,
but Christians cannot thereby reject as evil other manifestations of the
Lord in non-Christian cultures. Yet Christians do not have much experience of living with a Christ they regard as less than universally
normative. Since all truth is not disclosed, the universality of Christ is
as logically possible as a more relative position.

What Christians need to guard against is a loosening of their adherence to Christ as they understand Him. That human understanding is
relative does not eliminate responsibility to the particular understanding
a person has.

D. Historical Resonance

Throughout Christian history there has been a dialog with other traditions. In the early days of Christianity Hellenistic culture was both
friend and foe. Where Paul had to insist on the centrality of Christ,
later authors such as Clement of Alexandria and Justin Martyr, ac-
knowledged the wisdom of God touching all things and influencing
non-Christian philosophers. Even these early theologians regarded
Christian scriptures as normative when conflict with philosophical con-
clusions arose. The Middle Ages was a period in which the philosophies of Plato and Aristotle helped to provide frameworks for Christian
thought. While Christians, Moslems, and Jews were in tension and
even in war, their understandings of God were remarkably similar.
Christian theologians used Moslem and Jewish writings to advance
 ʾstian thought. As a result of Moslem conquest of southern Europe,

Christians and Moslems sometimes lived together and recognized each other as relating to God. In 1076 Pope Gregory II admitted that a Moslem could be saved through obedience to the Koran.[6] Despite the few examples of Church tolerance which historians can uncover, in general both the Roman and the Eastern Orthodox Churches felt sufficiently threatened by Moslem and Protestant inroads in Europe to be hostile rather than dialogical toward other religious traditions. The Second Vatican Council was a breakthrough in mutual respect between Roman Catholicism and people with different faith. Today especially in America the dialogs continue, along with shared spiritual practices across religious lines.

E. Method

The mutual benefit of inter-religious dialog is more than tolerance, though that is no small benefit. The arena of religious practice is where barriers are coming down. Throughout the United States there are many centers for religious practice that derive from Hinduism and Buddhism. Some of these centers encourage inter-religious sharing. It is not uncommon to find Catholic contemplative monks and nuns practicing yoga or transcendental meditation, and Christians can participate in Christian Zen retreats. The practices of another tradition can open up new experiences for Christians. They can also bring confusion which is an unavoidable risk that requires guidance by people rooted in their own tradition.

In addition to meditative practice, the reading of texts from other traditions can help people to awaken to values in their own tradition previously neglected. Think of Mohandas Gandhi, for example, who was inspired by the Sermon on the Mount in the New Testament. That inspiration helped him to advance non-violence in his own Hindu context, which also contained a commitment to non-violence. The same phenomenon has occurred in the other direction when many Christian peace activists have been inspired by the writing of this 20th century Hindu, Gandhi. By reading Gandhi's works, many Christians have passed over into sympathetic relationship with another tradition from their own and have returned to their own tradition with a heightened awareness of non-violence in the New Testament and early Christianity.[7] Today a Christian can easily learn from non-Christian traditions as well as from ancient and contemporary Christian sources.

F. Resources

Abhishiktananda, Swami. *Prayer*. Phila.; Westminster Press, 1972.

Dunne, John S. *The Way of All the Earth*. Notre Dame: University of Notre Dame Press, 1978.

Griffiths, Bede. *Christ in India*. N.Y.: Scribner, 1967.

Johnston, William. *The Still Point*. N.Y.: Fordham University Press, 1982.

Merton, Thomas. *The Asian Journal*. N.Y.: New Directions, 1973.

———. *Mystics and Zen Masters*. N.Y.: Farrar, Straus & Giroux, 1961.

———. *Zen and the Birds of Appetite*. N.Y.: New Directions, 1968.

Panikkar, Raimon. *Invisible Harmony*. Minneapolis: Fortress, 1995.

———. *The Trinity and the Religious Experience of Man*. N.Y.Orbis Books,1973.

Rahner, Karl. *Theological Investigations*, Vol.IX. N.Y.: Herder and Herder,1972.

———. *Theological Investigations*, Vol. XIV. N.Y.: Seabury, 1976.

NOTES

1. "Declaration on the Relation of the Church to Non-Christian Religions," Section 2 in *The Documents of Vatican II* (Westminster, Md.:The Newman Press, 1966); see also "Decree on the Missionary Activity of the Church." Section 9.

2. "Decree on the Missionary Activity of the Church," Section 9.

3. For Rahner on anonymous Christianity see Gerald McCool, *The Rahner Reader* (New York: Seabury Press, 1975), 211-224.

4. Panikkar, Raimundo, *The Trinity and the Religious Experience of Man* (New York: Orbis, 1973), 53: see P. Knitter, *No Other Name* (Maryknoll: Orbis, 1985), 153-7; see Knitter's book for both a summary of Pannikar's thought and an excellent survey of critical issues related to Christianity and world religions.

5. See Knitter, 185.

6. Theodore Robb and Jerome Seigel, *Action and Conviction in Early Modern_Europe* (Princeton, N.J.: Princeton University Press, 1969), 324 n.2.

7. See John Dunne, *The Way of All the Earth* (Notre Dame, Indiana: University of Notre Dame Press, 1978) for a discussion of this type of passing over.

III. Personalism: Thomas Merton

A. Historical Situation

The European West including western Europe and the United States had been experiencing enormous cultural self-confidence in the 19th century as colonial expansion demonstrated the apparent superiority of western civilization. In the beginning of the 20th century technological invention and industrial competence continued the sense of the destiny of the West to guide the rest of the world. This self-confidence was humiliated by World War One. There, civilized Europeans butchered and poisoned each other. The West was now uncertain. The carnage of World War Two further undermined the identity and direction of the western psyche. The darkness within has surfaced, and people no longer could count on science, technology, industry, and rationality to lead civilization into the twenty-first century.

In this climate a small but symbolically significant counter-culture movement grew. Within Catholicism contemplative monasteries flourished; in the late 1940s, one monk's autobiography became successful as a nation looked for spiritual refreshment and inspiration. *The Seven Storey Mountain* by Thomas Merton sold hundreds of thousands of copies in its first year of publication in 1948. Young men and women flocked to cloistered life to find a source of truth and love beyond the machinations of western technocrats, and many found in Merton's writings the articulation of their own deepest longings. In the 1950s the beat poets provided the foundation for the hippies of the 1960s; both movements looked to the Orient for spiritual nourishment. Merton helped traditionally conservative Catholics to turn to the depths of their own hearts and traditions as well as toward the wisdom of the East. Since we have already discussed Christianity in dialog with other relig-

ions, the focus here will be on Merton as link with one of the key insights of Christianity, the person.

Merton saw the person as the key to relationship with God and also
that which needed to be protected from technological society which
was more intent upon increasing production and consumption.

B. Contemplative Perspective

Christianity, in general, sees God as personal rather than as an Impersonal Absolute. What "personal" has historically implied is a relational
reality that is free and intelligent. This free and intelligent source of
reality cares about not only the lilies of the field but also about other
persons who, unlike flowers, can freely develop a conscious relationship with God. This understanding is at the heart of Christianity and is
symbolized by the term "Trinity," which denotes God as relational.
However one conceives of Trinity, the inescapable meaning is that the
Father as source of all is not isolated but communicative. The communication took human form in the Son, and the gift of the Son's relationship with the Father is given to humanity through the Holy Spirit.

Mainstream Christianity has maintained that God is free, that God
freely chose to create the world. In other words, all of creation is loved
into being. This love includes each person who is loved prior to having
done or having failed to do anything. People can come to an awareness
of God's unconditional love by looking in the mirror and considering
how it is that they exist rather than not. Existence points to its source, a
source that is free and intelligent. (If God were not free and intelligent,
not personal, then God would be less than some creatures. People do
not believe this-- that the Creator is less than creatures.)

Instead of basking in the unconditional love of God, people live as
though their existence needs to be earned. People can spend their lives
trying to earn approval by being kind, moral, religious, macho, efficient, pretty, or whatever and thinking these qualities will protect them
from being forgotten or ignored. People try to establish themselves in
the minds of others as though their existence depended upon those
minds. The illusion is that people will drop out of existence if some
others are not thinking about them. The further illusion is that people
have the capacity to establish themselves in existence. At most, people
can move their existence around, but the source is beyond them. If one
believes in life after death, people cannot even end their own existence.
Existence is a gift, but people often live as though they need to give
birth to themselves.   Instead of a gift, people regard existence as

something to be won by good performance; existence can even appear to be a matter of competition. Thus people sometimes step on others or put others down in order to affirm themselves. God's affirmation is ignored. To wake up to that affirmation is a central thrust of Christian preaching and teaching. Without an awareness of God's love, Christianity does not work, and human life may feel like a desperate climb.

Merton's perspective can be simplified through distinguishing two levels of human identity. The psychological identity is who I think I am. This experience of self is largely shaped by one's interactions with other people. If I live in an environment that is accepting, then I will think and feel well about myself. If the significant people in my life are unaffirming I am likely to have difficulties with self-acceptance and self-image.

The other level of self is one's theological identity which refers to who I am in relation to God. As Merton writes,

> Who am I? My deepest realization of who I am is -- I am one loved by Christ. This is a very important conception. It takes us below the mere level where I decide who I am by the reaction of persons to me. On the social level we create identities for one another by the way we treat each other. ...Expectations of other people are secondary...The depths of our identity is in the center of my being where I am known by God. ...The great central thing in Christian Faith and Hope is the courage to realize oneself and to accept oneself as loved by God even though one is not worthy. Identity does not consist in creating worthiness, because he loves us in any way. We know God loves us as we are.[1]

One's theological identity as one loved by God is largely unconscious. In general, people do not have continuous conscious communion with God. The fullness of personhood does not mean substituting psychological with theological identity which would be an impossible goal. Rather the way to full personhood would be to allow one's psychological identity to be informed and influenced by theological identity. As I increasingly experience myself as loved and accepted by God, my felt need to establish myself or to put others down will diminish. Of course this is a gradual process, but what is clear is that conscious relationship with God can impact relationships with oneself and others.

Here a Merton distinction will help. He distinguishes between person and individual, which the English language tends to see as synonymous. The person is an expression of being in relationship with God, being an image of God, whether conscious or not. The individual is who I am as contrasted with everyone else. An individual is simply an undivided being, but on the level of conscious experience the individual is the ego.

> People who know nothing of God and whose lives are centered on themselves, imagine that they can only find themselves by asserting their own desires and ambitions and appetites in a struggle with the rest of the world. They try to become real by imposing themselves on other people, by appropriating for themselves some share of the limited supply of created good and thus emphasizing the difference between themselves and the other men who have less than they, or nothing at all.
>
> They can only conceive one way of becoming real: cutting themselves off from other people and building a barrier of contrast and distinction between themselves and other men. They do not know that reality is to be sought not in division but in unity, for we are "members of one another."
>
> The man who lives in division is not a person but only an individual.[2]

The person is who I am in the eyes of God, which through prayer and Christian reflection I can make more conscious. Personhood thus is shared with everyone since all are loved by God. Individuality consists in difference, not in unity. If my conscious identity is composed entirely of how I differ from others, community will be difficult to find or establish. Sooner or later the personality differences of others will annoy. If, however, in my own conscious experience is an awareness of God's unconditional love, I have a fighting chance of relating to other people on that level. I can recognize the uniqueness of others as embraced by God, as I have been. To be person in Merton's sense implies God's creative love, and growth in personhood involves allowing relationship with God to influence relationship with self and others.

The personalism of Merton is not the cult of self that our culture has made famous. Individualism is not personalism. Individualism seeks self-aggrandizement; personalism expresses relationship with God, works for the common good, and protects the dignity of each person. To provide for the good of each person means that individual use of resources will yield to concerns broader than the self.

The mentality that is stuck in itself rather than in communion with God and others Merton calls "Cartesian." Cartesian consciousness is caught up in observing self and developing self-awareness over against objects. The increase of such self-consciousness gives knowledge of how the objects relate to self, hence the more control is given to the subject over against these objects. Thus the thinking subject over against all else becomes capable of manipulating others. While this type of awareness is valuable for making many decisions, it may lead to alienation and isolation.

> Modern man, in so far as he is still Cartesian...is a subject for whom his own self-awareness as a thinking, observing, measuring and estimating "self" is absolutely primary. It is for him the one indubitable "reality," and all truth starts here. The more he is able to develop his consciousness as a subject over against objects the more he can understand things in their relations to him and one another, the more he can manipulate these objects for his own interests, but also, at the same time, the more he tends to isolate himself in his own subjective prison, to become a detached observer cut off from everything else in a kind of impenetrable alienated and transparent bubble which contains all reality in the form of purely subjective experience. Modern consciousness then tends to create this solipsistic bubble of awareness--an ego-self imprisoned in its own consciousness, isolated and out of touch with other such selves in so far as they are all "things" rather than persons.[3]

Instead of relatedness one is left with detached observation, where other humans are reduced to objects. One even becomes an object to oneself: consider the contemporary fascination with self-analysis. God also becomes an object for those of us grasping for clear and distinct ideas. To have clear and distinct ideas about God, self, and others is not bad, but analysis is no substitute for communion. Ideas are not substitutes for personal presence.

Reflect how intimacy and presence may be blocked by categorization. Mary tells John about her trouble at work. He is receptive and truly listens. Uncomfortable with his friend's suffering, he pigeon-holes and offers a solution: "You are having trouble with your boss because he reminds you of your father who was distant. You need to free yourself from your father." The analysis may be true, but a friend is different from an analyst. Personal presence does not need to reduce the experience of another to manageable categories. Personal presence places a priority on just being.

On the level of relationship with God, theological refinement is valuable. To have ideas about God is a part of one's religious life, but theological study alone may not give the sense of God's presence available in prayer.

How free is a person to be present to God, self, others, and to the earth? Can I look at a field without wondering about its real estate possibilities? Can I meet another human being without reducing the other to my business, career, social, or sexual desires? Merton invites people to reflect on their freedom and personal presence.

The focus on the personal does not mean neglect of the social. Becoming one's truest self involves integration of knowledge through social interaction as well as prayer. This knowledge of one's connectedness flowers into a sense of social responsibility.

Merton's spiritual writing expanded beyond the cloister wall to include such issues as racism, militarism, and totalitarianism. Underlying these writings is a concern for persons who are subordinated to the values of production and consumption. Within the mass systems of contemporary society, persons themselves absorb the misleading imagery of advertising. In addition to the pressures from without to conform to the images of the good life to be found outside of oneself, human weakness embraces the illusion that having more and doing more lead to happiness.

Merton offers a metaphysical analysis of the human problem beneath the social problems of our time. "The real root-sin of modern man is that in ignoring and contemning being and especially his own being, he has made his existence a disease and an affliction."[4] The neglect of being is a problem of openness, an unwillingness to let fundamental questions and insights about one's existence emerge. One's being is mysterious, and mystery can be uncomfortable if not threatening to encounter. That I am raises the question of how. How is it that I am? This is a question that points to dependence which may burden one's sense of independence and perhaps diminish one's inflated feeling of autonomy.

Awareness of one's being increases the awareness of the being of all others. They in turn carry with them reminders of interdependence and limitation. To intuit the wonder of existing is to intuit one's origin in God's love.

Unable to rest in the embrace of Being, humans look with anxiety for happiness elsewhere. When such dis-ease drives people outside of themselves for bliss, they overlook the wonder of existence. Genuine happiness according to Merton consists in receiving self and reality as gifts, but no one is home to receive because they are outside on desolation row looking.

> It is precisely this illusion, that mechanical progress means human improvement, that alienates us from our own being and our own reality. It is precisely because we are convinced that our life as such is better if

we have a better can, a better TV set, better toothpaste, etc. that we condemn and destroy our own reality and the reality of our natural resources. Technology was made for man, not man for technology. In losing touch with being and thus with God, we have fallen into a senseless idolatry of production and consumption for their own sakes... We no longer know how to live, and because we cannot accept life in its reality life ceases to be a joy and becomes an affliction. And we even go so far as to blame God for it![5]

Mystical intimacy is the source of Merton's social concern; his approach to social issues does not come solely from an awareness of economics or politics but rather from a sense of the person.

C. Historical resonance

Merton's approach to Christian life is both practical and articulate. He lived in a highly structured monastic community which emphasized solitude. His thought tends to fall into the monastic theology of the Middle Ages where the journey to God was foremost. Throughout Christian history there have been those who aim to cultivate objectivity and precision. This type of theology is sometimes shaped by theological controversy (4th century Christology) or it may be shaped by a particular philosophical framework (Thomas Aquinas) or by a particular method (Abelard). Merton valued these theological traditions, but his own approach is more monastic and has more in common with the spirituality traditions of Christianity.

His approach to the person will illustrate his cultural rooting. If one studies the Christian concept of person, one will see Augustine, Boethius, Richard of St. Victor, Thomas Aquinas, and Duns Scotus as prominent in attempting to refine definition. One after another these writers examine the concept and try to cast their meaning into the available categories such as substance and accident. Without going into all of these writers here, a couple of high points will help.

Boethius, for example, in the context of Christological dispute defined person as an "individual substance of a rational nature."[6] His problematic was how to deal with unity and diversity in Christ who combines humanity and divinity in one package.

Prominent Christian writers such as Richard of St. Victor, Thomas Aquinas, and Duns Scotus tried with some success to improve on Boethius' definition which was flawed in that "person" meaning "individual" could not apply to both human and divine persons since the latter are not individuals. A twelfth century writer in Merton's Cistercian tradition takes another approach. For William of St. Thierry, person means image of God, and further person is a term that evokes the loving embrace of God.

The application of such categories as substance and accident might yield a notion of what a person is, but William's approach comes closer to the who of person, that is to an entrance into selfhood rather than whatness. According to William the Son of God "is in the bosom of the Father" (in sinu Patris); thus the Son "makes him known by an unspoken revelation." [7] Another translation shifts in sinu Patris to mean insinuation: "the only Son is the very insinuation of the Father, and thereby uncovers the Father in an unspeakable telling."[8] The Son is embraced by God, near to the heart of the Father in the bosom of the Father thus making the Father known or uncovered. In other words the Son insinuates the Father because the Son is embraced, is near to the heart of the Father. Not only can the Son reveal the Father as a result of being in intimate communion with the Father, so too can Christians. Thus William's approach to personhood is not so much a matter of definition, as it is an evocation of relationship with God.

Merton, like William of St. Thierry, approaches person as image of God as relatedness with God. Merton's approach does not give precise definition but rather evokes the possibility of relationship. This Merton accomplishes by speaking of true and false self, thus calling into question one's own identity and holding out God's call as focus for becoming one's true self.

To speak about imaging God in the manner of monastic and Cistercian theology implies a journey. Humans are born as images of God, but we have lost our likeness to God. We have fallen into the region of unlikeness and need to find the way back. This journey is the context of Merton's thought as well as that of Augustine, Bernard of Clairvaux, William of St. Thierry, and many of the monastic and patristic spiritual writers.

D. Christ: the One Mystical Person

Christ is the Word of God, and humans are called to echo that Word. "It is the gift of God Who, in His mercy, completes the hidden and mysterious work of creation in us by enlightening our minds and hearts, by awakening in us the awareness that we are words spoken in His One Word."[9] Human persons arise from within the Logos and image God in the world. Humans imaging God refers not only to origin but also to echoing God through human becoming: "...we ourselves are words of His. But we are words that are meant to respond to Him, to answer Him, to echo Him..." (p. 3)

The relationship that Christ has with the Father is the one to which human beings are called. In other words, through Christ humans share in God's relationship with His Son. This participation in Christ is without a gap since Christ bridges the gap between humanity and divinity. The unity with Christ is the basis for unity with all people who live in Christ.

> The Christian...is One with all his "brothers in Christ." His inner self is, in fact, inseparable from Christ and hence it is in a mysterious and unique way inseparable from all other I's who live in Christ, so that they all form one "mystical Person," which is "Christ."[10]

This "one mystical Person" is an acknowledgment of a communal reality in Christ. Here not only is the gap between divinity and humanity overcome but also that between the personal and the communal.

Awakening to this metaphysical union is the goal of consciousness. In the last talk Merton gave before his death, he described transformation of consciousness:

> In the process of this change the individual ego was seen to be illusory and dissolved itself, and in place of this self-centered ego came the Christian person, who was no longer just the individual but was Christ dwelling in each one. So in each one of us the Christian person is that which is fully open to all other persons, because ultimately all other persons are Christ.[11]

Merton's Christ is where the self of God and the self of humans meet; He is the Person in whom humans are embraced by God and called to fullness of life.

E. The Journey

Personhood according to Merton is a journey out of a region of unlikeness to God into union through self-transcending love of God and other people.

Unlikeness to God in Merton's writings implies a life dominated by self-preoccupation. Unable to discover and rest in God's love, people are haunted by anxiety: am I any good? Does anybody care? People need affirmation, and there is very little unconditional love available outside the love of God.

The journey to God is a journey through self-knowledge. Self-knowledge for Merton means a knowledge of self as image of God, as creature, and as sinner. To know self as loved image is to turn to God through whatever prayer method one finds helpful. Merton does not give a method; for himself the monastic environment helped to foster interiority. In addition Merton was nourished by liturgical prayer and meditative reading of sacred texts. All methods are in service of relationship. That statement does not eliminate the need for method (especially for those of us who live outside of monasteries), but it puts methods in their properly subordinate place.

Self as creature is self without an established place in existence independent of God. Dependence is a burden to the inflated ego, but ultimately dependence is a door to gratitude.

To know self as sinful is to accept that one has been unfaithful to one's values and commitments and that one is susceptible and vulnerable. To experience the fear of infidelity and self-disgust are common yet avoided. Self-disgust when rooted in recognition of sin helps to drive a person out of self into compassion. Without this kind of compunction or dread, one will not escape from a judgmental and contemptuous posture. Some years ago I was in an apartment in Harlem on New Year's Eve with friends. As midnight came the sound of celebrating voices filled the neighborhood. One of my friends missed the beauty of the mixing voices; instead he confessed that he hated their ignorant revelry. That moment of hatred became an important step in of my friend's religious conversion. Dread of self is filled with hope.

The struggle with self and the glory in God's presence fill Merton's writings. The language of self or of person for Merton is designed to lead to God; a person is a direct reference to God. Christianity is about this type of personalism: awakening to personal depth and fostering social relations that foster human dignity.

F. Sources

The most helpful books in appreciating Merton's personalism:

Merton, Thomas. *Contemplative Prayer.* N.Y.: Image Books, 1969.
———. *Love and Living.* N.Y.: Harcourt Brace Jovanovich, 1979.
———. *New Seeds of Contemplation.* N.Y.: New Directions, 1961.
———. *Zen and the Birds of Appetite.* N.Y.: New Directions, 1968.

My book *Merton and Walsh on the Person.* Brookfield, Wisconsin: Liturgical Publications, 1988 expands all of the above ideas on Merton.

NOTES

1. Thomas Merton, "A Conference on Prayer, Calcutta, October 27, 1968," *Sisters Today* 41 (April 1970): 452-453.

2. Thomas Merton, *New Seeds of Contemplation* (N. Y.: New Directions, 1961), 47-48

3. Thomas Merton, *Zen and the Birds of Appetite* (N.Y.: New Directions, 1968), 22

4. Thomas Merton, *Conjectures of a Guilty Bystander* (N.Y.: Image Books, 1968), 221.

5. 222.

6. Boethius, "A Treatise Against Eutyches," 3.4 in *The Theological Tractates*, translated by H.F. Stewart and E.K. Rand (Loeb Classical Library, N.Y.: G.P. Putnam's Son, 1926).

7. William of St. Thierry, *The Enigma of Faith* (Washington: Cistercian Publication, 1974), 2.

8. Thomas Tomasic, "William of St. Thierry: Toward a Philosophy of Intersubjectivity," (Ph.D. dissertation, Fordham University, 1972), 114.

9. *New Seeds of Contemplation*, 4-5.

10. Thomas Merton, "The Inner Experience," unpublished manuscript the Abbey of Gethsemani, 15; this manuscript has been published serially in *Cistercian Studies* in 1983 and 1984.

11. Thomas Merton, *The Asian Journal of Thomas Merton* (N.Y.: New Directions, 1973), 333-334.

IV. Revelation

A. Revelation through Creation, Soul, Scripture.

Comparative study of religion (thanks to Panikkar) yields two prominent themes within Christianity: person and word. As personalism was the focus of the last chapter, here we will examine God's self communication. The Word of God is a rich term that refers to the Bible, to messages within the Bible, to God's creative activity (Genesis 1), to God's message to the Biblical peoples, to God's guidance (Torah), or even to Jesus of Nazareth.

A great medieval Franciscan theologian, St. Bonaventure, captures the richness of the notion of God's word through the imagery of the book. Bonaventure as a Franciscan endorsed St. Francis' celebration of God through creation by referring to the Book of Creation. God, as any author, leaves vestiges of Himself in creation. If people learn to read the Book of Creation, they will intuit God. Without going into the Trinitarian speculations of Bonaventure, it is not uncommon for people to think of God when viewing the grandeur of a sunset or to speak of God when witnessing the awesome beauty of a mountain scene.

> Tiger, tiger, burning bright,
> In the forest of the night,
> What immortal hand or eye
> Could frame thy fearful symmetry. . .   (Blake)

In addition to seeing creation as a source of Divine revelation, Bonaventure sees the soul as a book for God's word. The functioning of the human soul carries the divine image, and that image pokes through in ways that imply God. A simple way in which the human soul images God is through human freedom which lifts humanity above the rest of creation. Since we are not totally tied to instinct, so too is God free in His creative activity. Christianity has long held that the world emerges from God's free choice rather than from necessity. Another

way in which human activity implies God is the restlessness of human
desire. The limitless craving for beauty, truth, and goodness images
God's infinity. These ways of finding God in humans self-confirm the
appropriateness of the metaphor of the Book of the Soul(see Cousins
and Whitson for the Bonaventure references).

If the Books of the Soul and of Creation contain God's revelation,
why do people not find God easily? Bonaventure and much of Christian tradition would say that the problem is one of human sinfulness.
Human perception is clouded by sin, and to help confused humanity,
God has given the Book of Scripture. The Book of Scripture speaks of
God in explicit terms which helps people to find God in themselves and
in the rest of creation.

B. Revelation as Objective

Two categories that theologians give to revelation are objective and
subjective. Since revelation as objective is familiar to Christian readers, I will begin with that understanding. A traditional view of revelation is that it is a matter of words and deeds. God reveals Himself
through events in history and through words to prophets.

The exodus from Egypt reveals God's saving intention; God liberated
the Hebrew people from slavery and led them through the desert to the
promised land. The Hebrew people interpreted these events as revela-
tory. God has shown His love through this liberation. The obvious
problem with this understanding is that interpretation is required for the
deeds to be revelation. Words are required to interpret God's deeds.
How much do the events carry revelation, or is not the interpretation
the key to revelation?

The other difficulty with this view is that deeds are ambiguous. The
Hebrews may have understood their exodus from Egypt through the
desert to the promised land as God's intention, but the people who were
already living in what later became Israel did not share that interpretation. For them the Hebrews were an invading force which wrought
destruction on their civilization. From the point of view of the Hebrews, the Canaanite view is wrong and vice versa. Is God on all sides
or not? Does revelation require that one take sides?

The revelation of God through words includes prophetic utterances.
A prophet is one who has a keen insight into what God wants to communicate to a community. Aside from this biblical understanding is a
popular meaning of prophet as associated with someone who can predict the future. This future element comes into play when one consid-

ers what prophets say. Prophets typically call people to realign their lives with God's will and stress how people have strayed from the right path. If people do not amend their ways, then calamities will ensue. This is the future component of many prophetic utterances.

Prophecy, legal decisions, prayers, narratives, proverbs all have entered into what Christians call revelation. These literary forms have entered the Bible, as part of revelation. Some authoritative church teaching is also considered to be revelation by most Christians. For example the first seven ecumenical councils have defined doctrines about God that summarize important Christian teaching. That God is one in three persons is not a biblical statement, but most Christians would say that it was revealed by God.

The Second Vatican Council accepts that revelation is a matter of words and deeds. Article 2 of "The Dogmatic Constitution on Divine Revelation" speaks of God's plan to reveal Himself: "This plan of revelation is realized by deeds and words having an inner unity: the deeds wrought by God in the history of salvation manifest and confirm the teaching and realities signified by the words, while the words proclaim the deeds and clarify the mystery contained in them."

The focus on revelation as objective is appropriate for Christianity in as much as it is based on the words and deeds of Jesus who lived in history and is not merely an archetype of human possibility.

C. Revelation as Subjective

Despite the objectivity of revelation, a balanced understanding of revelation includes a focus on the subjective pole. A person can have a pile of Bibles and have memorized the key doctrines of Christianity and yet manage to miss God's revelation. Jesus of Nazareth after all was prophetically challenging the understanding people had of God and of themselves. If Christian doctrine is reduced to information without challenge, then God's revelation is less than it might be.

Suppose a preacher faces a congregation and proclaims that "it is easier for a camel to go through the eye of a needle that for a rich man to be saved." (Mt.19:24) If the materially comfortable congregation hears no challenge or does not open the eyelid of their hearts to examine lifestyle and relationship to money, then revelation has not occurred (at least according to Rudolf Bultmann and to his followers). The interior challenge posed by the word of God makes revelation come alive.

If one looks at how the objective sources of revelation were composed, one may conclude that they are rooted in subjectivity. A prophet or Jesus Himself may strive to be attuned to God. This reaching out for God is an experience that all people share. Jesus, for example, gave a name to the end of his deep striving: *Abba*. Once he named the God to whom he was relating, that word could become a symbol that others could use in their inner exploration. The subjectivity of Jesus yields an objective symbol which in turn leads to the subjectivity of others.

Revelation emerges from subjectivity; it is objectified in some cases, and it leads back to subjectivity. Christian revelation includes historical events and the words and symbols of the past, but it is designed to influence human interiority.

D. The Bible and Revelation

1. Inspiration

Christians learn from the New Testament that the Bible is inspired by God: "All scripture is inspired by God." (1 Timothy 3:16) What exactly does this mean? Does each word come from God, and the evangelists engaged in automatic writing?

In an attempt to spell out how the Bible is inspired the Catholic Church under Leo XIII turned to Thomas Aquinas for the instrumental theory of inspiration. This states that God is the principal author of scripture, and humans are God's instruments. If the human instrument does not write well, the message is not communicated. This maintains God's part in the writing of the Bible but does not adequately explain the social nature of biblical composition.

Consider the differences between two versions of the same biblical story. Mark's account, which is likely to be earlier than Matthew's, emphasizes the lack of understanding of the disciples:

> . . . "Take heed, beware of the leaven of the Pharisees and the leaven of Herod." And they discussed it with one another, saying, "We have no bread." And being aware of it, Jesus said to them, "Why do you discuss the fact that you have no bread? Do you not yet perceive or understand? Are your hearts hardened? Having eyes do you not see, and having ears do you not hear? And do you not remember? When I broke the five loaves for the five thousand, how many baskets full of broken pieces did you take up?" And they said to him, "Seven." And he said to them, "Do you not yet understand." (Mark 8:14-21)

Matthew's version shows that the disciples do understand:

. . . "Take heed and beware of the leaven of the Pharisees and Sadducees." And they discussed it among themselves, saying, "We brought
no bread." But Jesus, aware of this, said, "O men of little faith, why do
you discuss among yourselves the fact that you have no bread? Do you
not yet perceive? Do you not remember the five loaves of the five
thousand, and how many baskets you gathered? How is it that you fail
to perceive that I did not speak about bread? Beware of the leaven of
the Pharisees and Sadducees." Then they understood that he did not
tell them to beware of the leaven of bread, but of the teaching of the
Pharisees and Sadducees." (Mt. 16: 5-12)

With one version saying the disciples understand and the other that
they do not understand, questions about God's involvement become
more complicated. How can both versions be true if they contradict
each other? Assuming that Matthew edited Mark's version, how could
Matthew change Mark's version if Matthew believed the earlier version
to be inspired by God?

Apparently Matthew has adjusted Mark's text to edit out some of the
emphasis on the lack of understanding of the disciples. Matthew is
establishing Church authority (see Matthew 16 and 18) and gives an
image of the apostles that is more flattering than the image given in
Mark's Gospel. Mark, on the other hand, stresses the difficulty of understanding the meaning of Jesus; the disciples' lack of understanding
ties in with that theme. In short, each evangelist shapes material about
Jesus to promote particular understandings.

Divine inspiration can be understood in terms of the material the
evangelists received as well as their editing of that material. The intelligence of the author, the audience he had in mind, the time and place
in which he wrote all influence the content of the biblical work. There
is no need to screen God out of this process, but God's revelation is
placed in human hands. Humans are influenced by God, and the social
and individual factors are part of the process. In other words inspiration may be understood through rather than in spite of human intelligence.

A balanced approach to the topic of Christian revelation involves a
dialog between objectivity and subjectivity. The mind of the believer
does not invent Jesus of Nazareth, but that mind selects elements from
the preached or written word that fit and make sense. The preached
and written word are "objective" in the sense that they are not projec-
tions from the heart of the believer, yet the heart of the believer needs
to be so disposed to accept what is written or preached.

2. Truth in the Bible

The question of Biblical truth historically is associated with the topic of inerrancy. With the advent of critical scholarship the notion of inerrancy requires serious qualifications.

Discovering what appear to be errors in the Bible is not difficult. Apparent errors can guide us to qualifying statements about discovering truth in the Bible.

Place the Bible in historical context. The Bible is not a science book; look for truth about relationship about God rather than an accurate description of the physical universe. The book of Genesis, for example, speaks of "windows of the heavens" (Gn. 7:11) The biblical authors did not have telescopes, and "windows" was a picturesque term to account for how the "waters above the heavens" reached earth.

Identify the literary form of the biblical passage under consideration. Establish whether the passage is poetry, prophecy, parable, narrative, saga, prayer or whatever. If a passage is a parable, for example, one would not ask historical questions of non-historical material. "The kingdom of heaven is like a woman who took leaven and hid it in three measures of meal." (Mt. 13) To ask the name of this woman or where she lived would be an absurd disregard for what type of literature a parable is. A parable is a metaphor or simile; it is not historical. Much of the Bible is not historical. This does not mean that a parable does not convey truth; parables convey truth by non-historical means.

To equate truth with history is too narrow for the Bible. The Adam and Eve story with the talking snake, tree of the knowledge of good and evil, and the tree of life can hardly be regarded as historical. Search for a tree of life, but one does not exist! I once had a biblical literalist say to me that the tree of life was extinct! Though the elements of the story of Adam and Eve are not historical, the story nevertheless teaches truth about human beings. Human beings like Adam and Eve want to have God's power to determine right and wrong; humans want that autonomy and strive for it by hiding from God. The story reveals this truth about humans even though the story is fiction.

3. Tradition

Tradition in Christian thought simply means what is handed on. Christian experience is handed on through texts and rituals and lifestyles. The word "tradition" became embroiled in controversy during the Protestant reformation when "tradition" was contrasted with "the Bible." This contrast overlooks the "handed on" nature of the Bible. The Bible emerges from Christian experience and is part of Christian tradition.

Tradition may be clarified by the concepts of "inner" and "outer" words of God. The people who lived with and interacted with Jesus encountered him as outside of themselves. Only those who were gifted with the inner word of God, meaning faith or the Holy Spirit, understood him to be a word from God. The inner word giving an enlightened understanding of Jesus yielded the outer word, namely the New Testament. This book is an outer word of God for generations later than that of Jesus. This book also requires the inner word for revelation to occur and for Christian experience to be "handed on." Thus tradition involves the dialog between the outer and inner words of God.

E. What is Revealed?

Christian awareness stretches between the historical and the symbolic, the unique and the recurring pattern. This is crucial for the topic of revelation as well as for Christian experience.

Often in Christian spirituality the theme emerges that happiness comes from within and that changing external circumstances will not necessarily change a person's experience of life. This conviction manifests in monastic detachment from society as well as in Platonically inspired interiority. Happiness comes from the inward turn toward God and away from chasing the created images of ultimate beauty, truth, and goodness.

This inward focus links with the patterns that Christianity endorses. When Paul suffered, he saw his suffering as part of the pattern of Christ (Philippians 3:9) and presented this as an opportunity for Christians (Philippians 1:29). Christianity offers Christians the pattern of dying and rising as a perennial possibility. This follows the Jewish practice of presenting the exodus from Egypt as part of a pattern available for Jews of all time.

The Christian promotion of patterns fits well with the Church's image of the Christ of faith. The Jesus of history, however, expresses the uniqueness of historical reality. This uniqueness challenges the relevance of Jesus for anyone else. Jesus lived in a particular time and place; what does his experience have to do with the particular experience of anyone else? The focus on patterns helps to bridge the gaps between the unique existence of different persons across time and space.

In making decisions people are caught between attempting to interpret their choices in terms of the perspective of recurring patterns versus the raw particularities of history. Psychological counselors will warn people about their repeating past errors in new relationships; such warning is warranted by the patterns people carry around. At the same time each new relationship or each new choice is unique and not reducible to any pattern. Human freedom deserves not to be tied too tightly to past patterning.

I recently played roulette. I would place chips on black or red and would watch my mind trying to intuit whether the ball would next land on a black or red number. I was doing my best to comfort myself by telling myself that the first color, red or black, to pop into my mind would represent some magical communication from beyond me to guide me to the right choice. I found myself both desiring this guidance and resisting it as I reflected that the movement of the ball was not controlled by any intelligent power. The ball would land on red approximately 50% of the time, whether I was interiorly attuned or not! Was I willing to face the historical bareness of chance or did I need the comfort of some hidden power or pattern?

Clearly, religion often favors the pattern approach to life. At the same time Jesus was known to challenge patterns. This is where the question of revelation emerges. Do Christian sources reveal comforting patterns or a witness to a pattern breaking unique historical person?

To answer "both" is safe but obscure. In the life of an individual, choices will rest upon alignment with cultural patterns and/or the unique components of a particular situation and existence. Revelation will support either emphasis depending on what one chooses to see as revealed. Clearly institutional churches will emphasize universal patterns. Jesus has been called the "concrete universal" so that the events of his particular life carry universal meaning. On the other hand, Christians will struggle with reconciling the particularity of their lives with the universality of Christian teachings.

The pattern approach may evoke criticism by those who strongly value history both in their own lives and in the study of Jesus. The emphasis in this polarity will determine the "what" of Christian revelation. Why did Jesus die? To save sinners is the pattern answer. Why did Jesus die? He was in the wrong place at the wrong time expresses the more historically oriented answer.

The tension between pattern and historical uniqueness will always be part of Christianity which attempts to deal with a God that transcends history and Jesus who is grounded in human history. The literary issues associated with the Bible are also not going to be dissolved by some great insight as the complexities of interpretation will continue to generate more questions than answers.

The twentieth century theologian who has had some success in refocusing the questions of revelation is Han Urs Von Balthasar. He was not particularly receptive to the critical questions of biblical scholars as he wanted to bring to light what he believed to be the heart of Christianity. For Balthasar love alone is worthy of belief. The love he means is that of a God who, though self-possessed and happy, nevertheless bends low and reaches into human existence to elevate those receptive to a love that comes from beyond themselves. While Teilhard, Rahner, and Lonergan pointed to the tendency within nature to transcend itself. Balthasar points to the love of God, expressed in the Incarnation that is astonishing in its unanticipated form. Who could have predicted that God would take on the form of a servant to embrace the needy and those turned away? (See for example Balthasar's *Love Alone*.) This is what Christianity reveals, and if some biblical scholarship should miss this, then the writings of Balthasar may serve as a corrective.

F. Resources

Brenneman, James. *Canons in Conflict*. N.Y.: Oxford U., 1997.

Kathyrn and Ewert Cousins. *How to Read a Spiritual Book:* N.Y.: Paulist Press, 1981.

Dulles, Avery. *Models of Revelation*. N.Y.: Doubleday, 1983.

O'Collins, Gerald. and D. Kendall. *The Bible for Theology*. N.Y.: Paulist, 1997.

Ward, Keith. *Religion and Revelation*. Oxford: Oxford University Press, 1994.

Whitson, Robley E. *The Coming Convergence of World Religions*. Newman Press, 1971

V. Jesus

Jesus is the focus of Christianity, the object of divine revelation, symbol of God, and exemplar of human life. Jesus is also at the center of controversy. He was a controversial figure for his contemporaries; church councils attempted to settle dogmatic disputes surrounding him; and theological uncertainty characterizes the contemporary scene.

A. Jesus and the New Testament

Primary access to understanding Jesus comes through the New Testament where early Christians portrayed the words, deeds, and career of Jesus.

1. The Message of Jesus

To simplify the variety of statements attributed to Jesus, I will focus on three prominent and authentic themes.

a. The Kingdom of God

When scholars view Jesus from within his historical context, two points are clear. First of all, Jesus preached about the ruling power of God or God's kingdom. Secondly, what he meant by the ruling power of God was in tension with what his contemporaries expected. The notion of ruling power or kingdom of God had a history in Israel, so that when Jesus spoke about this idea, he would have evoked various meanings in his audience.

Originally for Israel, God was king without a human representative. Israel wanted a human representative of God and came to see kings Saul, David, and Solomon as chosen by God. Israel believed that there would always be a descendant of David as ruler (2 Samuel 7:11-16). David was anointed with oil when he was inaugurated; he was a messiah (=anointed with oil). Future messiahs were expected to administer God's rule to the people of Israel, but many others except descendants of David ruled. The people of Israel were ruled by Assyrians, Persians, Greeks, and Romans. How could God be ruling through these foreign invaders?

While most Jews contemporaneous to Jesus or the New Testament did not belong to any party, the most influential groups include the Sadducees, Pharisees, Essenes, and Zealots; their ideas about life give points of contrast with Jesus.

The Sadducees constituted a group of priests who claimed to be descendants of Zadok, the high priest at the time of David. Their status was thus inherited, and inherited status implies accumulated wealth and power. As wealthy and powerful religious figures, the Sadducees would have been conservative as they had much to conserve. Religiously they shied away from oral interpretation of the Hebrew scriptures, and politically they cooperated with the occupying Roman forces. The Sadducees did not leave any writings, so knowledge about them is limited. The New Testament asserts that they did not believe in resurrection. The religious focus of the Sadducees is the Temple in Jerusalem, that sacred place toward which pious Jews turned in prayer from wherever they stood. These priests who supervised Temple worship would have had difficulty seeing in Jesus the answer to their prayers. For example, Jesus spoke of the kingdom of God as like leaven. Leaven for the Sadducees would have been an inappropriate symbol of the sacred; leaven was a sign of corruption. Leavened bread was excluded from Temple worship. Thus Jesus could hardly have been associated with liturgical purity.

The Pharisees, unlike the Sadducees, did not inherit their status. The Pharisees were simply pious Jews who wanted to find God in the events of daily life. They attempted to democratize religion by looking to the ordinary rather than to the Temple; they thus held that the family table was the table of the Lord (thanks to Pawlikowski for this). The Pharisees articulated how to love God throughout the day by specifying godly behaviors. Hence their writings contain legal prescriptions on how far to walk on the Sabbath and what to eat and what not. With their belief in resurrection, they were the closest group to the Christians. As rivals for the allegiance of the same population, Christian scripture depicts them in negative terms. The Pharisaic concern for religious law would have found no ally in Jesus who was known to have broken religious rules, for example in violating the Sabbath call for rest by picking grain on the Sabbath or healing a man with a withered hand on the Sabbath.

The Essenes lived apart from ordinary Jewish life. They believed that the Temple worship was corrupt since the proper lineage for high priests was not followed. They retreated to the desert in order to live a life of ritual purity. They awaited a change in Jerusalem when religious ritual would be restored to its pristine condition. It is not likely that the Essenes would have seen in Jesus a man from God as Jesus did not live apart but lived among tax collectors and sinners and visited the Temple.

The Zealots were those who believed God's rule could be established by military means. With guerilla tactics the Zealots killed Roman soldiers in hopes that a military victory would be a victory for God. Jesus can hardly be associated with violence.

These four groups of Jews all would have had blocks to seeing God's work and word in Jesus. What Jesus meant by God's ruling power not only does not fit very well into the expectations of his contemporaries, but it also serves as a challenge to the hearers of his parables.

The so-called parables of reversal give fairly easy access to the meaning Jesus probably conveyed.[1] The term "reversal" refers to the reversal of values that comes when a person encounters God's power.

The parable of the good Samaritan (Lk. 10) begins with a dialog between a lawyer and Jesus. The scribe asks about eternal life; he recites the law about loving God and neighbor but asks who is his neighbor. In response, Jesus tells the story about a person who was beaten up and left on the side of the road between Jerusalem and Jericho. A priest and also a Levite walk by and do not help the man in the ditch. Finally a Samaritan walks over to the person on the roadside and applies first aid; the Samaritan takes the man to an inn and leaves money for further care of the victim. Jesus asks the lawyer who is the neighbor to the man.

The lawyer would naturally identify with the priest and Levite as they are all part of the same religious establishment. The lawyer would not associate Samaritans with God's ruling power as the Samaritans had altered the Jewish religion. Some Jews looked with disdain at Samaritans, yet Jesus makes the Samaritan the hero of the story!

The lawyer either has to cling to his perspective or change to integrate Jesus' challenge. What is conventionally good, namely being a priest and Levite, here is portrayed as failing to be good. What is conventionally bad, a Samaritan, Jesus portrays as good. This parable exposes the limits of the lawyer and the limits of the hearers of the parable. These limits are the places for reversal of values and the opportunities for God to rule.

This same dynamic appears in such parables as the Pharisee and tax collector (Lk. 18), the rich man and Lazarus (Lk. 16), the dutiful versus the prodigal son (Lk. 15), and the friends versus the lame as wedding guests (Lk. 14). In each case the conventional mindset is challenged. The apparently good, that is the pious Pharisee, the rich man, the dutiful son, and the friends are shown to be less desirable than the apparently bad ones. The Pharisee was consumed with pride; the rich man lacked compassion; the dutiful son was filled with resentment, and the friends could repay the kindness. The less desirable people, the tax collector, Lazarus, the prodigal son, and the lame, turned out to be more desirable in Jesus' estimation. Jesus exposed through parables whatever were the conventional limitations to love and compassion; the ruling power of God chips away at these limitations.

The challenge of the kingdom is the dynamic that makes Jesus' notion of the kingdom difficult to define. When the kingdom is defined, the dynamic may be lost. Jesus was not teaching that one needed to be a tax collector, poor, prodigal, or lame to be part of the kingdom. For Jesus to challenge conventional values of his contemporaries as well as his failure to fit into first century expectations make his early death easy to understand.

b. *Abba*

Jesus' use of *Abba* continues to be regarded as an authentic expression of Jesus' special relationship with God. This word, *Abba*, comes from the Aramaic term for father. Though there is no evidence of Jewish usage of *Abba* to address God in the time of Jesus, there is not enough literature to support any strong assertion about such Jewish usage or lack thereof.[2] While the uniqueness of Jesus' utterance is open to question, the implication of Jesus' trust in and intimacy with God remains.

c. Moral Authority

The moral authority of Jesus comes through the sermon on the mount. There in chapters 5-7 of Matthew's gospel we see Jesus discussing the law of Moses(see anthology). In chapter 5 Jesus says that he has not come to abolish but to fulfill the law and then proceeds to itemize the changes he prefers. The pattern established in that chapter is to quote a passage from the Torah and then to change it. For example, Matthew portrays Jesus declaring, "You have heard that it was said to the men of old, "You shall not kill; and whoever kills shall be liable to judgment." Immediately following this quotation from Exodus, Jesus adds his change: "But I say to you that everyone who is angry with his brother shall be liable to judgment." The important words are "but I say to you" as these words place Jesus' authority above the Torah.

From the few words selected above, Jesus comes across as one who challenged ordinary assumptions, prejudices, and limitations. Furthermore he enjoyed a special intimacy with God and displayed an extraordinary confidence in his own moral judgment and authority.

2. Deeds

What did Jesus do? He preached, taught, healed, cast out demons, and ate with outcasts. These activities all contain offers of life. As we have just seen, his preaching and teaching call people to wake up to God's presence and power in their lives. The physical healings and exorcisms free people from physical and spiritual suffering. The association with outcasts offers freedom from social oppression. Jesus is life giver.

One of the more interesting questions concerning Jesus' activities involves his preaching. Was he an apocalyptic preacher? There are those who would point to Mark 13 which speaks of cosmic upheavals as an indication of Jesus' end of an era perspective. Apocalyptic literature generally includes a response to crisis hoping for a dramatic intervention by God who will resolve the current situation. This intervention issues an end to an era which scholars like to call eschatological from the Greek *eschaton* meaning end.

Jesus as apocalyptic teacher is a challenging concept. The main problem is sorting out what Jesus actually said about a dramatic Divine intervention and end of history. Scholars are simply divided and are likely to remain so concerning what he taught and his relationship to apocalyptic thought. How perfectly or imperfectly Jesus fits apocalyptic categories is an ongoing debate. However well he fits, it is difficult to completely remove Jesus from a context of apocalyptic thinking. Then the problem is to figure out how central apocalyptic thinking was to Jesus. Did he expect the end of the world soon, necessarily, or likely? If Jesus was wrong about the end of the world, what does this say about Jesus' knowledge and the veracity of his other teachings? The uncertainties associated with Jesus and apocalyptic at least can communicate the limitations of current understanding and also provide incentive to engage in further reading.[3]

3. Career

The career of Jesus links his words and deeds to his death and resurrection which have been the traditional focus of Christians. In ancient creeds we hear that "he was born of the Virgin Mary, suffered under Pontius Pilate, was crucified, died, and was buried." Nothing between birth and death managed to be included into the Apostles Creed. To ignore Jesus' life in favor of these mysteries of birth and death is to dehumanize him.

A solid starting point for the career of Jesus is his baptism which the gospels present as an inaugural event for Jesus' public ministry. I label it as "solid" because it is clearly an event that Christians would not have invented for two reasons. Firstly Jesus submits to a baptism of repentance, yet the people who assembled the New Testament believed Jesus to be without sin. Why then does he receive a baptism of repentance? Christians have sought to answer that question, but Christians would have had an easier time by not including this event. The second problem with the baptism is that Mark's Gospel places Jesus in a subordinate position to John. (Mk.1) This potentially embarrassing relationship is quickly repaired by later gospels. In Matthew's version, John acknowledges the inappropriateness of the scene, "I need to be baptized by you, and do you come to me?" (Mt. 3:14) Luke's Gospel says that Jesus was baptized but omits the mention of "by John" (contrast Lk. 3:21 with Mk. 1:9).

The baptism opens the way for Jesus' Galilean Ministry in which he heals and casts out demons and challenges religious leaders. This Galilean ministry includes such events as picking grain on the Sabbath and healing on the Sabbath. These events generate hostility which any intelligent Jew would have anticipated.

For some reason Jesus leaves Galilee and heads for Jerusalem. Why he does this is not entirely clear. Perhaps Jesus was escaping the rejection of the local population (Mk. 6:4), perhaps he was escaping the political aspirations for him held by some of the Galileans, perhaps the mismanagement of the Temple bothered him. Whatever the reason, the significant point is that Jesus' ministry was important to him. He locked horns with religious authorities over such issues as Sabbath law and treatment of lepers. The energy that such conflicts consume is ample demonstration of Jesus' resolve. He tried to make a difference in the lives of his contemporaries in Galilee, and he turned away, toward Jerusalem.

If Jesus challenged some of the rules of his religious tradition, he now chooses to go to that part of his land where the rule makers reside. He is not avoiding conflict. Jesus would have to know certain things about future possibilities. He would have known that John the Baptist met with a violent death, and John would have been perceived by the authorities as similar to Jesus. Jesus would also have known that both Roman and Jewish authorities had the power to execute people. Jesus could not have helped to have seen the likelihood of conflict and even violence in his future. He nevertheless set forth for Jerusalem.

In other words, whatever meaning Jesus had for his Galilean ministry, he now had to integrate death into his ministry. Schillebeeckx uses the last supper in Jerusalem to highlight Jesus' vision. At the last supper in the face of likely arrest, Jesus does not disband.[4] Instead he comforts and strengthens his disciples and anticipates life in God. (Lk.22:18) Jesus of Nazareth looked beyond death(see the Anthology).

The death of Jesus results from his challenge to the religious and political establishment. He reached beyond the comfort of his religious tradition to confront those who promoted such artificial divisions between people as Jew and Samaritan, healthy and leper, rich and poor. The meaning of these divisions for society did not mean for Jesus exclusion from God's love and acceptance. The death and resurrection of Jesus are central to Christian understanding of Jesus; these mysteries are also the subject of ongoing interpretation.

The simplest Christian interpretation of Jesus' resurrection is vindication by God of Jesus' mission. Jesus' reform of his religious tradition is worthy of careful consideration; he is not easily dismissed as a misguided religious fanatic.

4. Developing New Testament Understanding

Jesus as a prophet who had a special relationship with God left his followers with many unanswered questions about his identity. They looked to the Hebrew Scriptures in order to understand further who Jesus was.

a. Jesus as Messiah

Since Jesus is part of Jewish life, there was speculation about his identity in terms of Jewish heroes. He was variously identified with Elijah and an awaited messiah (Mk. 8). While Luke's gospel accepts some identification with Elijah in so far as both Jesus and Elijah displayed healing powers (compare Lk.7:11-17 with 1 Kg. 17:17-24). Elijah had a distasteful side, namely his use of violence against those he condemned; Luke distances Jesus from Elijah's history of casting fire upon people. (Contrast Lk. 9:54 with 2 Kg.1:9-16) A less ambiguous hero is one who has no history, namely an awaited messiah. As mentioned above, Jews associated political and religious problems with a future that included divinely chosen leadership, namely a messiah.

The gospels of Matthew, Mark, and Luke all separate Jesus from the political aspirations of Jesus' contemporaries. The passion predictions of these gospels would have discouraged any thought by Jesus' followers that he sought public office. (Mk. 8; Mt. 16; Lk. 9) John's gospel also brushes aside the role of Jesus as earthly king with his, "My Kingship is not of this world." (Jn. 19:36)

Aside from this clarification that Jesus is not the Jewish replacement for the Roman ruler, the gospels attach messianic hopes to Jesus. No gospel does this more thoroughly than Matthew whose first two chapters contain numerous references to fulfillment of prophecy. Luke's gospel interprets Jesus' death and resurrection in terms of God's plan for a messiah to suffer: "Was it not necessary that the Christ should suffer these things and enter into his glory." (Lk. 24) Luke and other early Christians join the notion of messiah with that of the suffering servant in Isaiah.

b. Suffering Servant

The servant of God in Isaiah is a Hebrew figure that either represents the nation of Israel or is a leader of Israel, hence possibly messiah. This servant of God heals by suffering for others (Is. 53), and this understanding opens the door to interpreting Jesus' death as something undergone for the sake of others. A martyr dies for others in so far as his or her cause will benefit others. Jesus is understood this way as well as in a mysterious way that his death affects the cosmic moral order. He is world redeemer in the minds of Christians.

c. Jesus as Wisdom

The New Testament portrays Jesus as master of life and the religious tradition of his day. He proclaims that the Sabbath was made for humans not humans for the Sabbath; in so doing he outsmarted contemporary religious authorities. With Jesus' authority came the reputation of wise man. The New Testament presents Jesus as the spokesperson for divine wisdom. "Therefore also the Wisdom of God said, 'I will send them prophets . . .'" (Luke 11:49) In Matthew's gospel Jesus is not simply spokesperson of divine wisdom but is identified with God's wisdom. "Therefore I send you prophets . . ." (Matthew 23:34). The wise man, Jesus, not only utters words of wisdom but so embodies wisdom through his life that he is identified with wisdom.

Eventually Christians linked Jesus with the personification of wisdom that appears in Hebrew scripture such as Proverbs 8. There wisdom is depicted as God's master craftsman who helps God with creation. This is a scriptural basis for the presentation of Jesus as the pre-existent Word of God in John's gospel. There the Word of God (God's words are words of wisdom.) which exists prior to human history takes human form in Jesus. (John 1) Jesus, the wise man, the one who embodies divine wisdom, is one with the wisdom that preceded human history and his own human form.[5]

For New Testament writers Jesus of Nazareth is a prophet who takes on the injustice of his day; he comes to people with healing presence of an intimate son and servant of God. His power over evil, over human hearts and minds embodies God's love and wisdom. Jesus' death demonstrates both his willingness to die for his convictions and also his connection to the conflict between good and evil operating in all people (Luke 23).

1. Patristic and Medieval Clarity

Jesus as embodiment of God's truth and goodness to the point of identification with God, jarred some Jewish sensitivities. John's gospel grapples with monotheism and a son of God who is one with God. In the next few centuries this issue continued to perplex Christians. The council of Nicaea in the fourth century attempted to protect the divinity of Christ by saying that Jesus is one being with the Father against the Arian claim that Jesus was a creature.

In the fifth century, the council of Chalcedon attempted to cap speculation by speaking of two natures, divine and human, united in one person in Christ. This type of doctrinal formula attempted to define the parameters of the discussion. While it helped to solidify Christian belief, the relationship of divinity and humanity in Jesus lost its context in the life and ministry of Jesus.

2. Spirituality beyond Doctrine

Despite the doctrinal perplexities over whom or what Jesus was, Christians continued to reverence, worship and imitate Jesus. The first few centuries of Christianity developed interiorly to the point where Jesus became an inner guide.

a. Inner Teacher: Clement of Alexandria and Augustine

While the New Testament presents Jesus as a teacher, John's gospel adds the idea of Jesus indwelling disciples (John 17:26). In the patristic period a number of writers join these two ideas and portray Jesus as inner teacher. Clement of Alexandria, for example, has written about Christ as the inner teacher and has a treatise on Christ as teacher. For Clement humans are images of God in that human reason images the divine *Logos*. Humans have lost their likeness to God and attain that likeness through a life of virtue. Progress moves to increase in freedom from domination by passion. The Divine Teacher, Christ, offers guidance as humans advance spiritually.

The *Logos* was a common concept in the Hellenistic world, and Clements's understanding was close to that of the Jewish philosopher, Philo. Philo and Clement both saw the *Logos* as the mind of God the immanent law of all things [6] and God's adviser.[7] What then is uniquely Christian in Clement's understanding of the *Logos*? What Lilla finds in Clement and not in any of Clement's non-Christian sources is the personal way the Logos intervenes in human life and transformation. The Logos "lovingly guides" Christians.[8] Into seekers, God "breathes . . . strength for the completion of their salvation."[9] The *Logos* is the Educator: "The Word . . . teaches all things and uses all things to educate us . . . man is reformed by the Word by whom He is tamed as though he were a wild beast."[10] The image of the intervention of the Word as taming a beast is strong, but coercion is not the way Clement understands the manner in which Christ works. Christ the Instructor educates, applies corrective discipline, and persuades.[11] Although Clement emphasizes the necessity of living according to reason, he sees such living as cooperation between the Christian and the *Logos*: "reason translated into deeds under the guidance of the educator."[12] Through the guidance of Christ the inner Teacher, humans are reshaped into the likeness of God.

b. Inner lover: Bernard

Next to the psalms, the Song of Songs is one of the most popular books of the Hebrew Bible for Christian meditation from Origen through the middle Ages. A number of the masters of Christian spirituality wrote commentaries on the Song of Songs. This love song between bride and bridegroom expressed the Christian experience of spousal love where Christ, the bridegroom is moved by love for the receptive bride, the Christian individually and/or communally as the Church.

Rather than a detailed analysis, I will offer an excerpt from the writing of the most prominent Christian mystical writer of the twelfth century, Bernard of Clairvaux. In Bernard's seventy fourth sermon on the Song of Songs, he describes the transforming presence of Christ the Bridegroom:

> You ask them how I know he was present, when his ways can in no way be traced. He is life and power, and as soon as he enters in, he awakens my slumbering soul; he stirs and soothes and pierces my heart, for before it was hard as stone, and diseased. So he has begun to pluck out and destroy, to build up and to plant, to water dry places and illuminate dark ones; to open what was closed and to warm what was cold; to make the crooked straight and the rough places smooth, so that my soul may bless the Lord, and all that is within me may praise his holy name. So when the Bridegroom, the Word, came to me, he never made known his coming by any signs, not by sight, not by sound, not by touch. It was not by any movement of his that I recognized his coming . . . Only by the movement of my heart . . . did I perceive his presence; and I knew the power of his might because my faults were put to flight and my human yearnings brought into subjection. I have marveled at the depth of his wisdom when my secret faults have been revealed and made visible; at the very slightest amendment of my way of life I have experienced his goodness and mercy; in the renewal and remaking of the spirit of my mind, that is of my inmost being, I have perceived the excellence of his glorious beauty, and when I contemplate all these things I am filled with awe and wonder at his manifold greatness.[13]

Here Christ, the inner lover, brings about changes in the life, thought, and affection of person receptive to him. This type of experience of inner transformation is Christ, the inner Christ who is to a large degree immune from the twentieth century scholarly preoccupation with the historical Jesus. Here Christ is an inner presence who profoundly affects the reformation of the deformed image of God in humans. This is also a Christ who is easily recognizable to praying Christians (as evidenced by the popularity of H. Hurnard's *Hinds Feet on High Places*, a contemporary allegorization of the Song of Songs).

As the quotation from Bernard of Clairvaux suggests, the inner Christ illuminates self-awareness by bringing to mind those things in need of attention. The inner Christ also touches human affection by inflaming desire for God and the works of God. The inner Christ is a presence of unconditional love which brings peace to those receptive to that love.

I offer the notion of Christ as inner reality to balance the objectivizing tendency of New Testament scholarship. Christ is the principal Christian object of revelation, yet as important for Christianity is Christ as interior guide and loving presence. The interior presence of God is typically called the Holy Spirit, but important classical voices of Christian spirituality acknowledge Christ as the One who works from within.

B. Contemporary Scene

a. History and Faith

Since the eighteenth century, New Testament scholars have been distinguishing what Jesus taught from what his followers taught. Scholars generally identify this distinction as the Jesus of history versus the Jesus of faith. This distinction is radical as it calls into question Christian understanding of what Jesus said and did. Consider the following text from Matthew's gospel where Jesus is presented as saying:

> If your brother sins against you, go and tell him his fault, between you and him alone . . . if he does not listen, take one or two others along with you . . . If he refuses to listen to them, tell it to the church; and if he refuses to listen even to the church, let him be to you as a Gentile and a tax collector. (Mt. 18)

Two problems emerge from this text. Firstly "church;" how can the disciples "tell it to the church" prior to the formation of church? This mention of church calls into question whether Jesus said these words and suggests that early Christianity placed these words in the mouth of Jesus to highlight church authority. The second problem is Jesus' use of the words "tax collector" to typify someone who is incorrigible. How could Jesus who was known to be a friend of tax collectors and even called one to belong to his intimate band of disciples, turn around and use "tax collector" in the sense of someone who is beyond help? Again the work of early Christianity is a likely explanation. Critical study of the New Testament uncovers many such problems with assuming that Jesus actually uttered this or that particular word. There are so many of these problems that New Testament scholarship assumes that there is no absolute certainty about any particular statements in the New Testament as actually coming from Jesus.

The Jesus of history would include those items in the New Testament that historical research could establish as likely to have come from Jesus. The Jesus of faith is the church's image of Jesus that is the developed image of Jesus. Whether that development is distortion or revelation is a separate question.

Despite the popularity of this distinction between faith and history, it implies the possibility of separating the Jesus of the Gospels from the Jesus of faith with any degree of certainty, and this is impossible. The Gospels are texts produced by people of faith and written to affect faith. Some passages may have greater likelihood than others of coming from Jesus, but the whole project is tentative. Jesus of history versus Jesus of faith is at best a distinction, not a separation, which may alert the reader to the important element of interpretation within the text. One may come to know interpretive characteristics, but freedom from all interpretation is not likely to be attainable.

Critical study is a response to genuine interest about what Jesus actually said and did. Recognition that the text is an amalgam of interpretations of the remembered Jesus, fuels interest and establishes a realistic level of expectation about what we can know at a distance of two millennia. What critical historical inquiry yields are probabilities[14] rather than certainties.

History, while dealing with unique and unrepeatable events, is limited to events in the past which are similar to present events. For example, historians as historians would not affirm the existence of virgin conception or a man walking on water because these types of events do not occur in the present. History is also limited to space and time. Events such as the rising from the dead and being seated at the right hand of the Father are beyond space and time. Historical limitations need to be distinguished from the Christian faith. Many of the most important items of Christian faith such as resurrection, divinity of Christ, and the existence of God do not fit within the limitations of history. This does not mean that these items are not true. What is called historical today is too narrow for Christian faith.

With the recognition of the limits of history, however, Christianity benefits from historical research in its understanding of Jesus. For example, the divisions between Jew and Samaritan that Jesus challenged are in conflict with the division between Christian and non-Christian that early Christianity established. Knowing Jesus' opposition to this type of artificial separation helps to free Christianity from elements that do not measure up to Jesus' standards.

What is the relationship between faith and history in research concerning Jesus? Three basic answers to this question summarize the work of numerous scholars.

First faith equals history, that is, faith is based on history. The problem with this position is that it needs to ignore or explain away the non-historical material in the Bible.

Second Faith is immune from history. This position holds that what matters in Christianity is the impact of the New Testament on the hearers or readers. The weakness of this position is that it does not protect Christianity from a purely mythological Christ. Most Christians believe Christianity has some rooting in historical events.

The third position called the "historical risk school" holds that faith and the Jesus of faith are primary within Christianity but that history plays a subordinate role. Historical knowledge does alter one's understanding of Jesus. Openness to historical knowledge involves a risk as the faith image may be enhanced or diminished by historical knowledge.[15]

Recall the baptism of Jesus by John the Baptist. As mentioned above, this story carries some embarrassment for Christianity and thereby helps to establish the historical authenticity of the event. Does that image of Jesus as undergoing a baptism for repentance diminish or enhance one's faith image?

3. Jesus' ministry and contemporary imagination.

The dominant model of Jesus in Christian history has been as the Incarnation of God. The early Christian creeds begin with his birth and immediately mention suffering and death. The Apostles' Creed says, he was ". . . born of the Virgin Mary. He suffered under Pontius Pilate."." As mentioned above the link between Jesus and wisdom enables early Christianity to understand Jesus as the Incarnation of the Son of God who existed beyond time and space. This understanding begins in God and then has to try to reconcile the less than God like activities of Jesus, namely lack of knowledge (Mt. 24:36), and temptation. How can a divine being not know everything and how can a divine being be pulled toward evil?

Divine attributes include omniscience and omnipotence, none of which fit the gospel portraits of Jesus. Instead a more Bible rooted approach might ask, what about God shines through what Jesus said and did?

Thought about Jesus that begins in God where the Son of God and the Father have a prior arrangement, wherein Jesus is supposed to go to earth to die. This makes Jesus' ministry relatively unimportant because the death of Jesus is believed to be the all important saving event. To balance this understanding, much of contemporary study of Christ focuses on his ministry. The assumption is that Jesus was not just treading water while waiting for Good Friday. On the contrary, Jesus was committed to his work and to making a difference in his society.

This focus on Jesus' ministry, which is firmly rooted in the New Testament, enables the humanity of Christ to emerge without having to justify itself. The humanity of Christ becomes the relevant focus for Christian attention. The words and deeds of Jesus in his ministry become opportunities for influencing Christian life.

The ministry of Jesus, which entails such things as embracing outcasts and challenging the misuse of power by religious authorities, receives development in modern cinema. Pasolini's "The Gospel of Saint Matthew" presents Jesus as an angry prophet who challenges the Jewish establishment. Scorsese's "The Last Temptation of Christ" shows the anguish of a Jesus who is torn between ordinary life and the challenge posed by Roman occupation of Israel and the conflict between the life of a prophet and ordinary family life. Denys Arcand's "Jesus of Montreal" depicts a troupe of actors who are commissioned to revise a worn-out passion play. The audience sees that the pattern of Christ manifests in the life of the actor who plays Jesus in the passion play. This actor accompanies one of the actresses in the play to an audition for a television commercial. She needs to earn money and presents herself to the director of the commercial. The director asks her to remove her sweater to expose her breasts, but she is hesitant. The actor who plays Jesus advises her to resist, and then Jesus-like he takes action to protect her dignity by smashing the camera. His prophetic intervention mirrors that of the Jesus of the gospels. These cinematic depictions of Christ are fictional, and yet they communicate images and words that are consistent with elements in the New Testament. These fictional accounts bring out the inner Christ of the filmmaker and connect with the inner Christ of the viewer. Thus the concern with historical study of Christ can help to bring to the forefront of Christian imagination the Christ who brings possibilities to human life. At the same time the inner Christ guides writers, filmmakers, and the Christian pub-

lic to discover and create new connections between themselves and the
Jesus of 2000 years ago.

C. Resources

Bernard of Clairvaux. *On the Song of Songs, Vol. IV.* Kalamazoo: Cis-
tercian Publications, 1980.
Cook, Michael. *The Jesus of Faith.* Ramsey, N.J.: Paulist Press, 1979.
Dunn, James D. G. *Christology in the Making.* Philadelphia: Westmin-
ster Press, 1980.
————. *Jesus Remembered*, Grand Rapids, Eerdmans, 2003.
Fuller, Reginald and Pheme Perkins. *Who is this Christ?* Philadelphia:
Fortress Press, 1983.
Meier, John. *Jesus A Marginal Jew, Vol. 2* Anchor Bible 1994.
O'Collins, Gerald. *Christology.* N.Y.: Oxford: Oxford University Press,
1995.
Pawlikowski, John T. *Christ in the Light of the Christian-Jewish Dia-
log.* Paulist, 1982.
Schillebeeckx, Edward. *Jesus.* N.Y.: Crossroads, 1979.
Vermes, Geza. *Jesus in his Jewish Context.* Fortress, 2003.

NOTES

1. John D. Crossan, *In Parables* (S.F.: Harper & Row, 1985), 53-78.

2. Geza Vermes, *Jesus in His Jewish Context* (Fortress, 2003), 38.

3. Worthwhile reading include Dale C. Allison , Marcus Borg, John Dominic Crossan, Stephen Patterson, *The Apocalyptic Jesus: A Debate.*   Polebridge Press 2001 ; Ehrman, Bart. *Jesus :Apocalyptic Prophet of the New Millenium.* Oxford U. Press, 1999; John Meier. *Jesus A Marginal Jew, Vol. 2* Anchor Bible 1994; E. Schillebeeckx. *Jesus.* N. Y.: The Seabury Press, 1979.

4. E. Schillebeeckx, *Jesus* (N.Y.: Crossroads, 1979), 306.

5. For further discussion of Jesus and wisdom see Fuller, R. and P. Perkins, *Who is this Christ?* (Philadelphia: Fortress, 1983), chapters 5 and 8 and James Dunn, *Christology in the Making* (Philadelphia: Westminster, 1980).

6. Clement of Alexandria, *Stromata* IV.155.

7. S. Lilla, *Clement of Alexandria* (N.Y.: Oxford U. Press, 1971), 201-208.

8. Clement, *Instructor* I.3.

9. *Stromata* VII.48.

10. *Instructor* III.99.

11. *Stromata* VII.6.

12.*Instructor* III.35.

13.Bernard of Clairvaux. *Sermons on the Song of Songs* 74.6.

14. James D. G. Dunn, *Jesus Remembered*(Grand Rapids, Eerdmans, 2003), 102.

15.See Michael Cook, *The Jesus of Faith* (New York: Paulist, 1981), chapter 1.

ANTHOLOGY

VI. Creation: Pierre Teilhard de Chardin Selections

[A Center of Convergence]

But in the Christian view only the eventual appearance, at the summit and in the heart of the unified world, of an autonomous centre of congregation is structurally and functionally capable of inspiring, preserving and fully releasing, within a human mass still spiritually dispersed, the looked-for forces of unanimisation. According to the supporters of this hypothesis only a veritable super-love, the attractive power of a veritable "super-being," can of psychological necessity dominate, possess and synthesize the host of other earthly loves. Failing such a centre of universal convergence, not metaphorical or potential but real, there can be no true coherence among totalised Mankind, and therefore no true consistence. A world culminating in the Impersonal can bring us neither the warmth of attraction nor the hope of irreversibility (immortality) without which individual egotism will always have the last word. A veritable Ego at the summit of the world is needed for the consummation, without confounding them, of all the elemental egos of Earth . . . I have talked of the "Christian view," but this idea is gaining ground in other circles. Was it not Camus who wrote in *Sisyphe*, "If Man found that the Universe could love he would be reconciled?" And did not Wells, through his exponent the humanitarian biologist Steele in *The Anatomy of Frustration*, express his need to find, above and beyond humanity, a "universal lover?"

Let me recapitulate and conclude.
Essentially, in the twofold irresistible embrace of a planet that is visibly shrinking, and Thought that is more and more rapidly coiling in upon itself, the dust of human units finds itself subjected to a tremendous pressure of coalescence, far stronger than the individual or national repulsions that so alarm us. But despite the closing of this vice nothing seems finally capable of guiding us into the natural sphere of our interhuman affinities except the emergence of a powerful field of internal attraction, in which we shall find ourselves caught from within. The rebirth of the Sense of Species, rendered virtually inevitable by the phase of compressive and totalising socialisation which we have now

entered, affords a first indication of the existence of such a field of unanimisation and a clue to its nature.

Nevertheless, however efficacious this newly born faith of Man in the ultra-human may prove to be, it seems that Man's urge towards Some Thing ahead of him cannot achieve its full fruition except by combining with another and still more fundamental aspiration-one from above, urging him towards Some One.

[Paris, 18 January, 1950]

From P. Teilhard de Chardin, *The Future of Man* (N.Y.: Harper & Row, 1964), 301-302.

[Movement Above and Ahead]

Now that we have realized this, let us try to define and describe the two modes - one simply rational, the other specifically Christian - in which the human swarm, by an instinctive and imperative choice, is adopting the road of the West: a mass movement which we can even now witness for ourselves.

At the psychological root of all mysticism there lies, if I am not mistaken, the more or less ill-defined need or magnetic power which urges each conscious element to become united with the surrounding whole. This cosmic sense is undoubtedly akin to and as primordial as the sense of sex; we find it sporadically very much alive in some poets or visionaries, but it has hitherto remained dormant, or at any rate localized (in an elementary and questionable form) in a number of Eastern centres. In recent times there has emerged in our interior vision a universe that has at last become knit together around itself and around us, in its passage through the immensity of time and space. As a result of this, it is quite evident that the passionate awareness of a universal quasi-presence is tending to be aroused, to become correctly adjusted and to be generalized in human consciousness. The sense of evolution, the sense of species, the sense of the earth, the sense of man: these are so many different and preliminary expressions of one and the same thirst for unification - and, it goes without saying, they all, by establishing a correct relation to the object that gives rise to them and stimulates them, conform to the Western type of spiritualization and worship. Contradicting the most obstinate of preconceived opinions, the light is on the point of appearing not from the East, but here at home, in the very heart of technology and research.

From this point of view, it is in the direction of a dynamic and progressive neo-humanism (one, that is, which is based on man's having become conscious of being the responsible axis of cosmic evolution) that a mysticism of tomorrow is beginning to assert itself as the answer to the new and constantly increasing needs of anthropogenesis. A common faith in a future of the earth is a frame of mind, perhaps even the only frame of mind, that can create the psychic atmosphere required for a spiritual convergence of all human consciousness: but can that common faith, in its merely natural form, constitute a religion that will be permanently satisfactory?. . . In other words, is not something more required to maintain the evolutive effort of hominization unimpaired and unfaltering to its final term, and to love it: does it not call for the manifest appearance and explicit intervention of the ultimate focus of biological involution? I believe that it does; and it is here that Christic faith comes in to take over from and to consummate faith in man.

Twice already we have met this supreme crown to both the phenomenon of man and the metaphysics of union - the mysterious figure of the parousiac or risen Christ, in whom the two linked processes of involution and pleromization are simultaneously consummated. In "Christ-Omega," the universal comes into exact focus and assumes a personal form. Biologically and ontologically speaking, there is nothing more consistent, and at the same time nothing bolder, than this identification we envisage, at the upper limits of noogenesis, between the apparently contradictory properties of the whole and the element. And it follows necessarily that, psychologically, there is nothing more miraculously fruitful, because, in this anticipated centre to the total sphere, attitudes and "passions" are able to meet and to be multiplied by one another, which in every other mental compass remain irreparably separate. "To lose oneself in the cosmic," "to believe in and devote oneself to progress;" "to love another being of the same sort as one's self;" such are the only relationships possible in a purely human ambience - and there they cannot but be independent of one another or even mutually exclusive. "To love (with real love, with a true love) the universe in process of formation, in its totality and in its details," "to love evolution" - that is the paradoxical interior act that can immediately be effected in the Christic ambience. For the man who has once thoroughly understood the nature of a world in which cosmogenesis, proceeding along the axis of anthropogenesis, culminates in a Christogenesis - for that man, everything, in every element and event of the universe, is bathed in light and warmth, everything becomes animate and a fit object for love and worship - not, indeed, directly in itself (as popular pantheism would have it) but at a deeper level than itself: that is, at the extreme and unique term of its development.

Once things are seen in this light, it is impossible to adhere to Christ without doing all one can to assist the whole forward drive. In that same light, too, communion becomes an impassioned participation in universal action; and expectation of the parousia merges exactly, as we saw earlier. . . with the coming of a maturity of man; and the upward movement towards the "above" combines harmoniously with the drive "ahead" . . . And from all this follows that Christian charity, generally presented as a mere soothing lotion poured over the world's suffering, is seen to be the most complete and the most active agent of hominization.

By Christian charity, in the first place, the reflected evolutive effort, whether considered in its individual parts or as one whole, is charged, as we have just said, with love: and that is the only way in which the full depths of its whole psychic reserves can be released.

By charity, again, the miseries of failure and vital diminishment - even these! - are transformed into factors of unitive excentration (by which I mean the gift to, and transition into, another greater than self): so that they cease to appear as a waste-product of creation and, by a miracle of spiritual superdynamics, they become a positive factor of super-evolution: the true and supreme solution of the problem of evil . . . Thereby, too, if the vast and formidably complex motor of evolution is to drive ahead under full power, without distorting a single working part, Christian mysticism, the higher and personalized form of the mysticism of the West, must be recognized by the thinking mind as the perfect energy for the purpose, the eminently appropriate energy. - And in that conclusion we have a most significant indication that nothing can prevent it from becoming the universal and essential mysticism of tomorrow.

A phenomenology of involution, leading up to the notion of super-reflection. A metaphysics of union, culminating in the figure of the universal-Christ. A mysticism of centration, summed up in the total and totalizing attitude of a love of evolution. Super-humanity crowned by a super-Christ, himself principle of super-charity. Such are the three coherent and complementary aspects under which the organic oneness of a convergent universe is made manifest to us intellectually, emotionally, and in our practical activity.

[Paris, 12 August 1948]

[Communion through Action]

Each one of our works, by its more or less remote or direct effect
upon the spiritual world, helps to make perfect Christ in his mystical
totality. That is the fullest possible answer to the question: How can
we, following the call of St. Paul, see God in all the active half of our
lives? In fact, through the unceasing operation of the Incarnation, the
divine so thoroughly permeates all our creaturely energies that, in order
to meet it and lay hold on it, we could not find a more fitting setting
than that of our action.

To begin with, in action I adhere to the creative power of God; I coincide with it; I become not only its instrument but its living extension.
And as there is nothing more personal in a being than his will, I merge
myself, in a sense, through my heart, with the very heart of God. This
commerce is continuous because I am always acting; and at the same
time, since I can never set a boundary to the perfection of my fidelity
nor to the fervour of my intention, this commerce enables me to liken
myself, ever more strictly and indefinitely, to God.

The soul does not pause to relish this communion, nor does it lose
sight of the material end of its action; for it is wedded to a creative effort. The will to succeed, a certain passionate delight in the work to be
done, form an integral part of our creaturely fidelity. It follows that the
very sincerity with which we desire and pursue success for God's sake
reveals itself as a new factor-also without limits-in our being knit together with him who animates us. Originally we had fellowship with
God in the simple common exercise of wills; but now we unite ourselves with him in the shared love of the end for which we are working;
and the crowning marvel is that, with the possession of this end, we
have the utter joy of discovering his presence once again.

All this follows directly from what was said a moment back on the
relationship between natural and supernatural actions in the world.
Any increase that I can bring upon myself or upon things is translated
into some increase in my power to love and some progress in Christ's
blessed hold upon the universe. Our work appears to us, in the main, as
a way of earning our daily bread. But its essential virtue is on a higher

level: through it we complete in ourselves the subject of the divine union; and through it again we somehow make to grow in stature the divine term of the one with whom we are united, our Lord Jesus Christ.
Hence whatever our role as men may be, whether we are artists, work-
ing-men or scholars, we can, if we are Christians, speed towards the
object of our work as though towards an opening on to the supreme
fulfillment of our beings. Indeed, without exaggeration or excess in
thought or expression-but simply by confronting the most fundamental
truths of our faith and of experience-we are led to the following observation: God is inexhaustibly attainable in the totality of our action.
And this prodigy of divinisation has nothing with which we dare to
compare it except the subtle, gentle sweetness with which this actual
change of shape is wrought; for it is achieved without disturbing at all. .
. the completeness and unity of man's endeavour.

The Christian Perfection of Human Endeavour

There was reason to fear, as we have said, that the introduction of
Christian perspectives might seriously upset the ordering of human
action; that the seeking after, and waiting for, the kingdom of heaven
might deflect human activity from its natural tasks, or at least entirely
eclipse any interest in them. Now we see why this cannot and must not
be so. The knitting together of God and the world has just taken place
under our eyes in the domain of action. No, God does not deflect our
gaze prematurely from the work he himself has given us, since he presents himself to us as attainable through that very work. Nor does he
blot out, in his intense light, the detail of our earthly aims, since the
closeness of our union with him is in fact determined by the exact fulfillment of the least of our tasks. We ought to accustom ourselves to
this basic truth till we are steeped in it, until it becomes as familiar to us
as the perception of shape or the reading of words. God, in all that is
most living and incarnate in him, is not far away from us, altogether
apart from the world we see, touch, hear, smell and taste about us.
Rather he awaits us every instant in our action, in the work of the moment. There is a sense in which he is at the tip of my pen, my spade,
my brush, my needle-of my heart and of my thought. By pressing the
stroke, the line, or the stitch, on which I am engaged, to its ultimate
natural finish, I shall lay hold of that last end towards which my innermost will tends. Like those formidable physical forces which man con-
trives to discipline so as to make them perform operations of prodigious
delicacy, so the tremendous power of the divine attraction is focused on

our frail desires and microscopic intents without breaking their point. It sur-animates; hence it neither disturbs anything nor stifles anything. It sur-animates; hence it introduces a higher principle of unity into our spiritual life, the specific effect of which is--depending upon the point of view one adopts-either to make man's endeavour holy, or to give the Christian life the full flavour of humanity.

The Sanctification of Human Endeavour

I do not think I am exaggerating when I say that nine out of ten practising Christians feel that man's work is always at the level of a "spiritual encumbrance." In spite of the practice of right intentions, and the day offered every morning to God, the general run of the faithful dimly feel that time spent at the office or the studio, in the fields or in the factory, is time taken away from prayer and adoration. It is impossible not to work-that is taken for granted. Then it is impossible, too, to aim at the deep religious life reserved for those who have the leisure to pray or preach all day long. A few moments of the day can be salvaged for God, yes, but the best hours are absorbed, or at any rate cheapened, by material cares. Under the sway of this feeling, large numbers of Catholics lead a double or crippled life in practice: they have to step out of their human dress so as to have faith in themselves as Christians-and inferior Christians at that.

What has been said above of the divine extensions and God-given demands of the mystical or universal Christ, should be enough to demonstrate both the emptiness of these impressions and the validity of the thesis (so dear to Christianity) of sanctification through fulfilling the duties of our station. There are, of course, certain noble and cherished moments of the day-those when we pray or, receive the sacraments. Were it not for these moments of more efficient or explicit commerce with God, the tide of the divine omnipresence, and our perception of it, would weaken until all that was best in our human endeavour, without being entirely lost to the world, would be for us emptied of God. But once we have jealously safeguarded our relation to God encountered, if I may dare use the expression, "in his pure state " (that is to say in a state of being distinct from all the constituents of the world), there is no need to fear that the most trivial or the most absorbing of occupations should force us to depart from him. To repeat: by virtue of the Creation and, still more, of the Incarnation, nothing here below is profane for those who know how to see. On the contrary, everything is sacred to the men who can distinguish that portion of chosen being which is subject to Christ's drawing power in the process of consummation. Try, with God's help, to perceive the connection-even physical and natural-which binds your labour with the building of the kingdom of heaven; try to realise that heaven itself smiles upon you and, through your works, draws you to itself; then, as you leave church for the noisy streets, you will remain with only one feeling, that of continuing to immerse yourself in God. If your work is dull or exhausting, take refuge in the inexhaustible and becalming interest of progressing in the divine life. If your work enthrals you, then allow the spiritual impulse which matter communicates to you to enter into your taste for God whom you know better and desire more under the veil of his works. Never, at any time, " whether eating or drinking," consent to do anything without first of all realising its significance and constructive value in Christo Jesu, and pursuing it with all your might. This is not simply a commonplace precept for salvation: it is the very path to sanctity for each man according to his state and calling. For what is sanctity in a creature if not to adhere to God with the maximum of his strength?-and what does that maximum adherence to God mean if not the fulfillment-in the world organised around Christ -of the exact function, be it lowly or eminent, to which that creature is destined both by natural endowment and by supernatural gift?

Within the Church we observe all sorts of groups whose members are vowed to the perfect practice of this or that particular virtue: mercy, detachment, the splendour of the liturgy, the missions, contemplation. Why should there not be men vowed to the task of exemplifying, by their lives, the general sanctification of human endeavour?-men whose common religious ideal would be to give a full and conscious explanation of the divine possibilities or demands which any worldly occupation implies-men, in a word, who would devote themselves, in the fields of thought, art, industry, commerce and politics, etc., to carrying out in the sublime spirit these demands-the basic tasks which form the very bonework of human society? Around us the "natural" progress which nourishes the sanctity of each new age is all too often left to the children of the world, that is to say to agnostics or the irreligious. Unconsciously or involuntarily such men collaborate in the kingdom of God and in the fulfillment of the elect: their efforts, going beyond or correcting their incomplete or bad intentions, are gathered in by him " whose- energy subjects all things to itself." But that is no more than a second best, a temporary phase in the organisation of human activity. Right from the hands that knead the dough, to those that consecrate it, the great and universal Host should be prepared and handled in a spirit of adoration.

May the time come when men, having been awakened to a sense of the close bond linking all the movements of this world in the single, all-embracing work of the Incarnation, shall be unable to give themselves to any one of their tasks without illuminating it with the clear vision that their work-however elementary it may be-is received and put to good use by a Centre of the universe.

When that comes to pass, there will be little to separate life in the cloister from the life of the world. And only then will the action of the children of heaven (at the same time as the action of the children of the world) have attained the intended plenitude of its humanity.

[written in China between November 1926 and March 1927]

VII. Christianity and World Religions Selections

[The following selections from Karl Rahner speak, in sometimes challengingly long sentences, of the distinction between subjective openness toward the infinite as "transcendental knowledge" and the objectification of that openness in the word "God." This distinction allows Rahner to describe openness to God as a kind of "faith" despite the lack of the categories of Christianity in a person's mind. To surrender to truth is a surrender to God; the willingness to follow conscience is a type of faith as it is uncertain where truth will lead.]

How could it be possible for there to be an anonymous Christian?

Now how can we conceive of this possibility of faith in the "pagan?" In attempting . . . to answer this question . . .[notice] the difference and the unity between objective knowledge and that which is known on the one hand, and a non-objective, non-thematic awareness . . . on the other. . . . If we take these concepts . . . the theory of the possibility of personal faith in a "pagan" makes two assumptions: (1) The supernatural grace of faith and justification offered by God to men does not need to be conceived of as an isolated intervention on God's part at a particular point in a world which is itself profane. On the contrary it can perfectly well be interpreted on the basis of God's universal will to save as a grace which, as offered (!), is a constantly present existential of the creature endowed with spiritual faculties and of the world in general, which orientates these to the immediacy of God as their final end, though of course in saying this the question still remains wholly open of whether an individual freely gives himself to, or alternatively rejects, this existential which constitutes the innermost dynamism of his being and its history, an existential which is and remains continually present. God's universal will to save objectifies itself in that communication of himself which we call grace. It does this effectively at all times and in all places in the form of the offering and the enabling power of acting in a way that leads to salvation. And even though it is unmerited and "supernatural" in character, it constitutes the innermost *entelecheia* and dynamism of the world considered as the historical dimension of the creature endowed with spiritual faculties. It does not need to be consciously and objectively known as a dynamism of this kind, and even without such knowledge it is still present. (2) This grace constantly implanted in the nature of the creature and the historical dimension belonging to it as the dynamism and finalization of the history of man is, however, something of which man is aware in the manner in which such a reality does impinge upon human awareness. This awareness does not ipso facto or necessarily imply an objective awareness; it is present in the a priori formal objects, in the further levels of significance in the spiritual and intentional capacities of knowledge and freedom. Whether man explicitly recognizes it or not, whether he can or cannot reflect upon it in itself and in isolation, man is, in virtue of the grace offered him and implanted in him as his freedom in the mode of a formal object and of a spiritual perspective of an a priori kind, orientated towards the immediacy of God as his final end.

Atheism and Implicit Christianity

. . . we can draw up a sort of table of the fundamental types of man's relationship with God. In doing so it must always be borne in mind that a conscious or known reality present to man's mind may exist in the mode of free acceptance or free rejection, since man is not merely a being who is intellectually knowing, but is also always a free being.

First possibility: God is present in man's transcendental nature and this fact is objectified in a suitably and correctly explicit and conceptual theism, and moreover is also freely accepted in the moral affirmation of faith (in the practice of living). In this case we have what constitutes simply correct theism, what we might call transcendental and categorial theism, accepted and affirmed by man's freedom in both these dimensions. In this way it represents in every respect a proper relationship between man and God such as we may assume in the case of a justified Christian.

Second possibility; Both transcendental and categorial theism are present, man knows of God in his transcendental experience and also his reflection upon the latter is correct, but in his moral freedom he rejects this knowledge, whether as a sinner, denying God, or going on to reject the God whom he has correctly "objectified" conceptually in real free unbelief. This is the category in which the "atheist" was thought of previously in religious and in specifically Christian matters. It was assumed that he had an objectified and more or less correct idea of God but rejected him in sin or freely turned away from him either in a merely practical "godlessness" or in theoretical atheism as well.

Third possibility: The transcendental experience of God is present of necessity and is also freely accepted in a positive decision to be faithful to conscience, but it is incorrectly objectified and interpreted. This inadequate, false (and under certain circumstances totally lacking) idea of God as such can be again the object of free acceptance or rejection in various ways, but we need not concern ourselves with that in any greater detail here. For instance, consider the case of a polytheist who, in the dimension of free reflection, freely "believes" this polytheism or freely and "atheistically" rejects it, without replacing it by a correctly conceived theism. In either case this third instance is the sort of atheism which is innocent in the sense of Vatican II. It is atheism on the plane of categorical reflection, coexisting in the subject with a freely affirmed transcendental theism. There can be such a thing as innocent atheism because of the difference between subjective transcendentality and categorial objectification in concepts and sentences, producing this coexistence of transcendental theism and categorial atheism. For the said "difference" is necessarily present in every act of the mind. The components of this innocent atheism are: on the one hand the subject's continual transcendental dependence on God and the free acceptance of this dependence, especially in the moral act which respects absolutely the demands of conscience i.e. a transcendental theism "in the heart's depths" - and on the other hand the free rejection of the objectified concept of God, i.e. a categorial atheism in the forefront of conscious reflection, a rejection which cannot in itself be regarded as culpable.

Fourth possibility: The transcendental dependence on God is present; objectively it is interpreted falsely or insufficiently correctly in a categorial atheism, and this transcendental dependence on God is itself simultaneously denied in a free action by gravely sinful unfaithfulness to conscience or by an otherwise sinful, false interpretation of existence (as being "totally absurd" or of no absolute significance, etc.). In this case the free denial does not refer merely to the categorial interpretation of man's transcendental nature, but to existence and thus to God himself. Here we have culpable transcendental atheism, which excludes the possibility of salvation as long as it persists.

By presenting these four basic types of man's relationship with God we do not wish to suggest that the table could not have been drawn up differently, especially as we ourselves have indicated further subordinate possibilities within this "system." Furthermore, by naively distinguishing the correct from the false conceptual objectification of man's necessary transcendental dependence on God we have made an oversimplification which does not correspond to concrete reality. For here there are naturally correct and less correct conceptualisations (e.g. an idea of God revealing partially false, pantheistic or polytheistic tendencies and blemishes). Indefinite transitions and fluid boundaries are also compatible with the exercise of freedom. So the system we have outlined is no more than a rough preliminary sketch. But it may be sufficient for our purposes all the same.

[Panikkar rejects the notion that humans have an absolute point of view by which all religions can be comprehended. He sees each religion as unique and each having the potential to enrich the understanding of the seeker. He represents the pluralism position in the relationship between relations, and he counsels trust over suspicion and superiority.]

Dialogical Openness

Once internal dialogue has begun, once we are engaged in a genuine intrareligious scrutiny, we are ready for what I call the imparative method-that is, the effort at learning from the other and the attitude of allowing our own convictions to be fecundated by the insights of the other. I argue that, strictly speaking, comparative religion, on its ultimate level, is not possible, because we do not have any neutral platform outside every tradition whence comparisons may be drawn. How can there be a no-man's-land in the land of Man? In particular fields this is indeed possible, but not when what is at stake is the ultimate foundations of human life. We cannot compare (*comparare*-that is, to treat on an equal-par-basis), for there is no fulcrum outside. We can only *im-parare*-that is, learn from the other, opening ourselves from our standpoint to a dialogical dialogue that does not seek to win or to convince, but to search together from our different vantage points. It is in this dialogue, which cannot be multitudinous, but only between a few traditions in each case, where we forge the appropriate language to deal with the questions that emerge in encounter. Each encounter creates a new language.

In these dialogues we do not come up with great universal theories, but with a deepened mutual understanding among, say, Catholic Christianity and Saivasiddhanta, or between Lutheranism and Shi'ah Islam, or between modern Western philosophical categories and traditional Bantu religiousness. Once a net of relationships has been developed, it is relatively easy to establish new and more general links and even venture common categories. The great religions of Africa should be mentioned here, for they offer a peculiar difficulty on the one hand, and a grand facility on the other, to dialogue. It is difficult because often dialogue becomes doctrinal, abstract, metaphysical, and the genius of many an African religion lies elsewhere. We have difficulty in finding common categories. It is easy, on the other hand, because of the charge of humanity and concreteness of such exchanges. The common language is the simplest one.

These mutual studies, relationships, and dialogues change both the opinion of the one partner and the interpretation of the other. Religions change through these contacts; they borrow from each other and also reinforce their respective standpoints, but with less naivety. This type of dialogue is not only a religious endeavor for the participants, it is a genuine *locus theologicus*, to speak in Christian Scholastic parlance, a source in itself of religious (theological) understanding. A theory of a particular religion today has also to deal with other religions. We can no longer ignore the other. The religions of others-our neighbors-become a religious question for us, for our religion.

In a way, there is many a theory of religion claiming to be a universal theory of religion. But then we are, although on a second and much more fruitful higher spiral, at the same initial point-namely, having to confront a series of universal theories of religion. We will have to deal with, say, how Islam sees itself in the religious mosaic of our times, or how Marxism confronts the Hindu interpretation of reality.

This process of mutual learning has no end. Imparative religion is an open process. A universal theory attempts to clarify everything as neatly as possible in one single place and ends eventually by stifling any ultimate dialogue. In my alternative the polarities remain and the ideal is not seen in a universal theory, but in an ever emerging and ever elusive myth that makes communication, and thus mutual fecundation, possible without reducing everything to a single source of intelligibility or to mere intelligibility. The very theory is dialogical. In a word, the dialogical character of being is a constitutive trait of reality. Agreement means convergence of hearts, not just coalescence of minds. There is always place for diversity of opinions and multiplicity of mental schemes of intelligibility.

Human Cosmic Trust

What I am trying to put forward is not a counter-theory, but a new innocence. We should beware of so many reform systems that began with a greater universalistic impulse than the original systems and became new philosophies, new sects, or new religions. Often they do not subsume or even enhance the others but simply multiply their number. This may be not bad-except they do not achieve what they started to do. Any universal theory will soon become another theory.

We should beware of claiming to understand religions better than they have understood themselves. I do not deny this possibility, but it should carry along some contemporary representatives of such a religion, and at least partially transform that religion, lest our interpretation become a new religion. Religious traditions have more existential than doctrinal continuity. There are not many doctrines in common between a Christian of the first century and a present day one, for instance. The case of Hinduism is still clearer. Hinduism is an existence, not an essence. The decisive factor is the existential confession, not the doctrinal interpretation.

The study of religion, I repeat, is not like the scientific approach to physical phenomena, which even in the sciences is becoming obsolete. We are not dealing with objective facts-supposing they existed. Even in the case of allegedly revealed facts, we are still dealing with human constructs, which house, as it were, a group of human beings, giving them the housing of a more or less coherent and protective universe.

In our days we feel, perhaps more acutely than at other times, that we do not know each other, that we still mistrust one another, that in fact we are at loggerheads in many fundamental insights of immediate importance for the praxis of our lives. We are painfully aware of our differences because we are more conscious of our mutual existence and the need to intermingle-brought about by the techniculture of our times.

But we cannot chop off our divergences to remain only with what we have in common: we all want to eat and to be happy. This is fundamental, but hunger has many causes and the ways to happiness, and even its concept, differ.

Religions can no longer live in isolation, let alone in animosity and war. Traditional religions nowadays are not, by and large, very powerful and thus do not present a major threat, except of course in some countries. More secular religious ideologies today have greater virulence and fight each other. They cannot be left out of the picture in a discourse about the encounter of religions. The last two world wars were not strictly religious, and yet they were "theological." Where do we turn for harmony and understanding?

The political and economic situation of the world today compels us to radical changes in our conception of humanity and the place of humanity in the cosmos. The present system seems to be running toward major catastrophes of all kinds. This situation brings near the thought that if the change has to be radical and lasting, it also has to transform our ways of thinking and experiencing reality. The point in case of the religious traditions could not be more pertinent. I am prepared to argue that if there is any solution to the present predicament, it cannot come out of one single religion or tradition, but has to be brought about by collaboration among the different traditions of the world. No single human or religious tradition is today self-sufficient and capable of rescuing humanity from its present predicament. We can no longer say "that's your problem! " Hinduism will not survive if it does not face modernity. Christianity will disappear if it does not meet Marxism. Technocratic religion will destroy itself if it does not pay heed to, say, the Amerindian tradition, and so on. Humanity will collapse if we do not gather together all the fragments of the scattered cultures and religions. But togetherness does not necessarily mean unity, nor is understanding absolutely required.

What is needed is trust, a certain trust that sustains a common struggle for an ever better shaping of reality. I mean something like this. As the very word suggests (especially in Latin-*fiducia*), this "trust" entails a certain "fidelity" to oneself, "con-fidence" in the world as cosmos, "loyalty" in the struggle itself, and even (as perhaps etymologically hinted at) an attitude rooted in the soil of reality like a "tree," a basic "belief" in the human project, or rather in the worthwhile collaboration of humans in the overall adventure of being. It excludes only the suicidal and negative desire of self-destruction and annihilation of everything. It does not eliminate the passionate thrust toward the victory of one's own ideals-reprehensible as this may appear to many of us if this is striven for as an absolute.

Elsewhere I have proposed the distinction between the basic and constitutive human aspiration by which the human being is constituted as a human being, and the desires that plague concrete human existence when walking on the path toward realization. This, I would submit, takes into account the Buddhist criticism of *tanha,trsna*, thirst, desire, the one-pointedly Hindu concern for realization, and the Christian preoccupation with dynamism and creativity. There is a primordial human aspiration, but there are equally hasty desires. The trust I am speaking of is related to the human aspiration by which humans believe that life is worth living, because Reality can-must-be trusted.

The danger in this aspiration-in our case, we may say, toward truth-is that it can become a desire for our own understanding. In other words, the danger lies in the possible confusion between our desire to understand everything, because we assume (a priori) that reality is (should be) intelligible, and the aspiration of making sense of our life and all reality. This latter is the trust that there is some sense (direction, "meaningful" dynamism) in the universe.

This assumption is not a universal theory, not even a universal praxis. It is only so far a relative cultural invariant inasmuch as exceptions are seen precisely as aberrant deviations by the vast majority of mortals. This trust is an impulse simply not to give up in the task of being what we are (or should be), which some may say is that of being human, others divine.

Half a century ago I called this cosmic trust the cosmological principle, and millennia before it was called *rta, tao, ordo*. Even when we formulate the ultimate metaphysical question, "Why is there something rather than nothing?" we are assuming that the question is meaningful-that it is a real question-even if we do not find an answer, or only a nihilistic one. It may be said of this ultimate ground that there is something somewhere asking whether it all makes sense at all, or that it is all the dream of a dreamer and has never existed outside that dream, or that it is a very weak ground indeed for the unfolding of the universe and our participation in it. Yet it may be enough, for in one way or another we have to stop somewhere. Traditionally this ultimate ground has been called God, Man, or World. We have further interpreted those words as meaning consciousness, goodness, power, intelligence, nothingness, absurdity, matter, energy, and the like. We may change words and interpretations, but some fundamental trust indeed persists.

The ultimate ground for this cosmic confidence lies in the almost universal conviction that reality is ordered-in other words, is good, beautiful, and true. It is a divine Reality, say most of the human traditions. There is no need to blow up a wretched universe, because Reality is not evil ultimately. We may have to bring it to completion, to achieve it, as the fundamental principle of alchemy puts it, and eventually correct it, but not create an artificial-mechanical universe that we must have under control because we cannot trust Reality. Underlying this felt need for control there is a certain Protestant climate that "creation" is a fiasco, combined with some "humanistic" interpretation that the redeemer is Man. But Christian theology will tell us that redemption entails an inner dynamism that ultimately belongs to the "economic Trinity."

Reprinted by permission of the author from *Invisible Harmony: Essays on Contemplation and Responsibility* by Raimon Panikkar, edited by Harry James Cargas, copyright ©1995 Augsburg Fortress, 172-177.

[The historical complexity concerning the relationship between Catholicism and world religions here finds amicable and simple expression in an official statement by the Roman Catholic Church from the Second Vatican Council. The Church recognizes truth and holiness of God shining forth in non-Christian religions; this is a foundation that opens doors to respect.]

1. In our time, when day by day mankind is being drawn closer together, and the ties between different peoples are becoming stronger, the Church examines more closely her relationship to non-Christian religions. In her task of promoting unity and love among men, indeed among nations, she considers above all in this declaration what men have in common and what draws them to fellowship.

One is the community of all peoples, one their origin, for God made the whole human race to live over the face of the earth. One also is their final goal, God. His providence, His manifestations of goodness, His saving design extend to all men, until that time when the elect will be united in the Holy City, the city ablaze with the glory of God, where the nations will walk in His light.

Men expect from the various religions answers to the unsolved riddles of the human condition, which today, even as in former times, deeply stir the hearts of men: What is man? What is the meaning, the

aim of our life? What is moral good, what sin? Whence suffering and
what purpose does it serve? Which is the road to true happiness? What
are death, judgment and retribution after death? What, finally, is that
ultimate, inexpressible mystery which encompasses our existence:
whence do we come, and where are we going?

2. From ancient times down to the present, there is found among
various peoples a certain perception of that hidden power which hovers
over the course of things and over the events of human history; at times
some indeed have come to the recognition of a Supreme Being, or even
of a Father. This perception and recognition penetrates their lives with
a profound religious sense.

Religions, however, that are bound up with an advanced culture have
struggled to answer the same questions by means of more refined concepts and a more developed language. Thus in Hinduism, men con-
template the divine mystery and express it through an inexhaustible
abundance of myths and through searching philosophical inquiry. They
seek freedom from the anguish of our human condition either through
ascetical practices or profound meditation or a flight to God with love
and trust. Again, Buddhism, in its various forms, realizes the radical
insufficiency of this changeable world; it teaches a way by which men,
in a devout and confident spirit, may be able either to acquire the state
of perfect liberation, or attain, by their own efforts or through higher
help, supreme illumination. Likewise, other religions found every-
where try to counter the restlessness of the human heart, each in its own
manner, by proposing "ways," comprising teachings, rules of life, and
sacred rites.

The Catholic Church rejects nothing that is true and holy in these
religions. She regards with sincere reverence those ways of conduct
and of life, those precepts and teachings which, though differing in
many aspects from the ones she holds and sets forth, nonetheless often
reflect a ray of that Truth which enlightens all men. Indeed, she proclaims, and ever must proclaim Christ, "the way, the truth, and the life"
(John 14, 6), in whom men may find the fullness of religious life, in
whom God has reconciled all things to Himself.

The Church, therefore, exhorts her sons, that through dialogue and
collaboration with the followers of other religions, carried out with
prudence and love and in witness to the Christian faith and life, they

recognize, preserve and promote the good things, spiritual and moral,
as well as the sociocultural values found among these men.

3. The Church regards with esteem also the Moslems. They adore the one God, living and subsisting in Himself, merciful and all-powerful, the Creator of heaven and earth, who has spoken to men; they take pains to submit wholeheartedly to even His inscrutable decrees, just as Abraham, with whom the faith of Islam takes pleasure in linking itself, submitted to God. Though they do not acknowledge Jesus as God, they revere Him as a prophet. They also honor Mary, His virgin mother; at times they even call on her with devotion. In addition, they await the day of judgment when God will render their deserts to all those who have been raised up from the dead. Finally, they value the moral life and worship God especially through prayer, almsgiving and fasting. Since in the course of centuries not a few quarrels and hostilities have arisen between Christians and Moslems, this sacred synod urges all to forget the past and to work sincerely for mutual understanding and to preserve as well as to promote together for the benefit of all mankind social justice and moral welfare, as well as peace and freedom.

4. As the sacred synod searches into the mystery of the Church, it remembers the bond that spiritually ties the people of the New Covenant to Abraham's stock.

Thus the Church of Christ acknowledges that, according to God's saving design, the beginnings of her faith and her election are found already among the Patriarchs, Moses and the prophets. She professes that all who believe in Christ-Abraham's sons according to faith-are included in the same Patriarch's call, and likewise that the salvation of the Church is mysteriously foreshadowed by the chosen people's exodus from the land of bondage. The Church, therefore, cannot forget that she received the revelation of the Old Testament through the people with whom God in His inexpressible mercy concluded the Ancient Covenant. Nor can she forget that she draws sustenance from the root of that well-cultivated olive tree onto which have been grafted the wild shoots, the Gentiles. Indeed, the Church believes that by His cross Christ Our Peace reconciled Jews and Gentiles, making both one in Himself.

The Church keeps ever in mind the words of the Apostle about his kinsmen: "Theirs is the sonship and the glory and the covenants and the law and the worship and the promises; theirs are the fathers and from them is the Christ according to the flesh" (Rom. 9, 4-5), the Son of the Virgin Mary. She also recalls that the Apostles, the Church's main-stay and pillars, as well as most of the early disciples who proclaimed Christ's Gospel to the world, sprang from the Jewish people.

As Holy Scripture testifies, Jerusalem did not recognize the time of her visitation, nor did the Jews, in large number, accept the Gospel; indeed not a few opposed its spreading." Nevertheless, God holds the Jews most dear for the sake of their Fathers; He does not repent of the gifts He makes or of the calls He issues-such is the witness of the Apostle." In company with the Prophets and the same Apostle, the Church awaits that day, known to God alone, on which all peoples will address the Lord in a single voice and "serve him shoulder to shoulder" (Soph. 3, 9).

Since the spiritual patrimony common to Christians and Jews is thus so great, this sacred synod wants to foster and recommend that mutual understanding and respect which is the fruit, above all, of biblical and theological studies as well as of fraternal dialogues.

True, the Jewish authorities and those who followed their lead pressed for the death of Christ, still, what happened in His passion cannot be charged against all the Jews, without distinction, then alive, nor against the Jews of today. Although the Church is the new people of God, the Jews should not be presented as rejected or accursed by God, as if this followed from the Holy Scriptures. All should see to it, then, that in catechetical work or in the preaching of the word of God they do not teach anything that does not conform to the truth of the Gospel and the spirit of Christ.

Furthermore, in her rejection of every persecution against any man, the Church, mindful of the patrimony she shares with the Jews and moved not by political reasons but by the Gospel's spiritual love, decries hatred, persecutions, displays of anti-Semitism, directed against Jews at any time and by anyone.

Besides, as the Church has always held and holds now, Christ underwent His passion and death freely, because of the sins of men and out of infinite love, in order that all may reach salvation. It is, therefore, the burden of the Church's preaching to proclaim the cross of Christ as the sign of God's all-embracing love and as the fountain from which every grace flows.

5. We cannot truly call on God, the Father of all, if we refuse to treat in a brotherly way any man, created as he is in the image of God. Man's relation to God the Father and his relation to men his brothers are so linked together that Scripture says: "He who does not love does not know God" (I John 4, 8).

No foundation therefore remains for any theory or practice that leads to discrimination between man and man or people and people, so far as their human dignity and the rights flowing from it are concerned.

The Church reproves, as foreign to the mind of Christ, any discrimination against men or harassment of them because of their race, color, condition of life, or religion. On the contrary, following in the footsteps of the holy Apostles Peter and Paul, this sacred synod ardently implores the Christian faithful to "maintain good fellowship among the nations" (1 Peter 2, 12), and if possible, to live for their part in peace with all men, so that they may truly be sons of the Father who is in heaven.

From the "Declaration on the Relation of the Church to Non-Christian Religions" in *The Teachings of the Second Vatican Council* (Westminster, Maryland: The Newman Press, 1966), 267-272.

VIII. Personalism: Thomas Merton Selections

[Merton on Personal Identity]

Do not depend on the hope of results. When you are doing the sort of work you have taken on, essentially an apostolic work, you may have to face the fact that your work will be apparently worthless and even achieve no result at all, if not perhaps results opposite to what you expect. As you get used to this idea you start more and more to concentrate not on the results but on the value, the rightness, the truth of the work itself. And there too a great deal has to be gone through, as gradually you struggle less and less for an idea and more and more for specific people. The range tends to narrow down, but it gets much more real. In the end, it is the reality of personal relationships that saves everything.

There is no point in building our lives on this personal satisfaction, which may be denied us and which after all is not that important.

The next step in the process is for you to see that your own thinking about what you are doing is crucially important. You are probably striving to build yourself an identity in your work, out of your work and your witness. You are using it, so to speak, to protect yourself against nothingness, annihilation. That is not the right use of your work. All the good that you will do come not from you be from the fact that you have allowed yourself, in the obedience of faith, to be used by God's love. Think of this more, and gradually you will be free from the need to prove yourself, and you can be more open to the power that will work through you without your knowing it.

From Thomas Merton in a letter to James Forest dated Feb. 21, 1966, quoted in James H. Forest, "Merton's Peacemaking," *Sojourners* (December, 1978), 18.

What Contemplation Is Not

The only way to get rid of misconceptions about contemplation is to experience it. One who does not actually know, in his own life, the nature of this breakthrough and this awakening to a new level of reality cannot help being misled by most of the things that are said about it.

For contemplation cannot be taught. It cannot even be clearly explained. It can only be hinted at, suggested, pointed to, symbolized. The more objectively and scientifically one tries to analyze it, the more he empties it of its real content, for this experience is beyond the reach of verbalization and of rationalization. Nothing is more repellent than a pseudo-scientific definition of the contemplative experience. One reason for this is that he who attempts such a definition is tempted to procede psychologically, and there is really no adequate psychology of contemplation. To describe "reactions" and "feelings" is to situate contemplation where it is not to be found, in the superficial consciousness where it can be observed by reflection. But this reflection and this consciousness are precisely part of that external self which "dies" and is cast aside like a soiled garment in the genuine awakening of the contemplative.

Contemplation is not and cannot be a function of this external self. There is an irreducible opposition between the deep transcendent self that awakens only in contemplation, and the superficial, external self which we commonly identify with the first person singular. We must remember that this superficial "I" is not our real self. It is our "individuality" and our "empirical self" but it is not truly the hidden and mysterious person in whom we subsist before the eyes of God. The "I" that works in the world, thinks about itself, observes its own reactions and talks about itself is not the true "I" that has been united to God in Christ. It is at best the vesture, the mask, the disguise of that mysterious and unknown "self" whom most of us never discover until we are dead. Our external, superficial self is not eternal, not spiritual. Far from it. This self is doomed to disappear as completely as smoke from a chimney. It is utterly frail and evanescent. Contemplation is precisely the awareness that this "I" is really "not I" and the awakening of the unknown "I" that is beyond observation and reflection and is incapable of commenting upon itself. It cannot even say "I" with the assurance and the impertinence of the other one, for its very nature is to be hidden, unnamed, unidentified in the society where men talk about themselves and about one another. In such a world the true "I" remains both inarticulate and invisible, because it has altogether too much to say-not one word of which is about itself.

Nothing could be more alien to contemplation than the *cogito ergo sum* of Descartes. "I think, therefore I am." This is the declaration of an alienated being, in exile from his own spiritual depths, compelled to seek some comfort in a proof for his own existence(!) based on the observation that he ... thinks." If his thought is necessary as a medium through which he arrives at the concept of his existence, then he is in fact only moving further away from his true being. He is reducing himself to a concept. He is making it impossible for himself to experience, directly and immediately, the mystery of his own being. At the same time, by also reducing God to a concept, he makes it impossible for himself to have any intuition of the divine reality which is inexpressible. He arrives at his own being as if it were an objective reality, that is to say he strives to become aware of himself as he would of some "thing" alien to himself. And he proves that the "thing" exists. He convinces himself: "I am therefore some thing." And then he goes on to convince himself that God, the infinite, the transcendent, is also a "thing," an "object," like other finite and limited objects of our thought!

Contemplation, on the contrary, is the experiential grasp of reality as subjective, not so much "mine" (which would signify "belonging to the external self") but "myself" in existential mystery. Contemplation does not arrive at reality after a process of deduction, but by an intuitive awakening in which our free and personal reality becomes fully alive to its own existential depths, which open out into the mystery of God.

For the contemplative there is no *cogito* ("I think") and no *ergo* ("therefore") but only *SUM,* I Am. Not in the sense of a futile assertion of our individuality as ultimately real, but in the humble realization of our mysterious being as persons in whom God dwells, with infinite sweetness and inalienable power.

Obviously contemplation is not just the affair of a passive and quiet temperament. It is not mere inertia, a tendency to inactivity, to psychic peace. The contemplative is not merely a man who likes to sit and think, still less one who sits around with a vacant stare. Contemplation is much more than thoughtfulness or a taste for reflection. Certainly, a thoughtful and reflective disposition is nothing to be despised in our world of inanity and automatism-and it can very well dispose a man for contemplation.

From *New Seeds of Contemplation* by Thomas Merton, copyright ©1961 by the Abbey of Gethsemani, Inc. Reprinted by permission of New Directions Publishing Corp., 6-9.

What am I? I am myself a word spoken by God. Can God speak a word that does not have any meaning?

Yet am I sure that the meaning of my life is the meaning God intends for it? Does God impose a meaning on my life from the outside, through event, custom, routine, law, system, impact with others in society? Or am I called to create from within, with him, with his grace, meaning which reflects his truth and makes me his "word" spoken freely in my personal situation? My true identity lies hidden in God's call to my freedom and my response to him. This means I must use my freedom in order to love, with full responsibility and authenticity, not merely receiving a form imposed on me by external forces, or forming my own life according to an approved social pattern, but directing my love to the personal reality of my brother, and embracing God's will in its naked, often unpenetrable mystery. I cannot discover my "meaning" if I try to evade the dread which comes from experiencing my meaninglessness!

By meditation I penetrate the inmost ground of my life, seek the full understanding of God's will for me, of God's mercy to me, of my absolute dependence upon him. But this penetration must be authentic. It must be something genuinely lived by me. This in turn depends on the authenticity of my whole concept of my life, and of my purposes. But my life and aims tend to be artificial, inauthentic, as long as I am simply trying to adjust my actions to certain exterior norms of conduct that will enable me to play an approved part in the society in which I live. After all, this amounts to little more than learning a role. Sometimes methods and programs of meditation are aimed simply at this: learning to play a religious role. The idea of the "imitation" of Christ and of the saints can degenerate into mere impersonation, if it remains only exterior.

It is not enough for meditation to investigate the cosmic order and situate me in this order. Meditation is something more than gaining command of a Weltanschauung (a philosophical view of the cosmos and of life). Even though such a meditation seems to bring about resignation to God's will as manifested in the cosmic order or in history, it is not deeply Christian. In fact, such a meditation may be out of contact with the deepest truths of Christianity. It consists in learning a few rational formulas, explanations, which enable one to remain resigned and indifferent in the great crises of life, and thus, unfortunately, it may make evasion possible where a direct confrontation of our nothingness is demanded. Instead of a stoical acceptance of "providential" decrees and events, and other manifestations of "law" in the cosmos, we should let ourselves be brought naked and defenceless into the center of that dread where we stand alone before God in our nothingness, without explanation, without theories, completely dependent upon his providential care, in dire need of the gift of his grace, his mercy and the light of faith.

We must approach our meditation -realizing that "grace," "mercy" and "faith" are not permanent inalienable possessions which we gain by our efforts and retain as though by right, provided that we behave ourselves. They are constantly renewed gifts. The life of grace in our hearts is renewed from moment to moment, directly and personally by God in his love for us. Hence the "grace of meditation" (in the sense of "prayer of the heart") is also a special gift. It should never be taken for granted. Though we can say it is a "habit" which is in some sense permanently present to us, when we have received it, yet it is never something which we can claim as though by right and use in a completely autonomous and self-determining manner according to our own good pleasure, without regard for God's will though we can make an autonomous use of our natural gifts. The gift of prayer is inseparable from another grace: that of humility, which makes us realize that the very depths of our being and life are meaningful and real only in so far as they are oriented toward God as their source and their end.

When we seem to possess and use our being and natural faculties in a completely autonomous manner, as if our individual ego were the pure source and end of our own acts, then we are in illusion and our acts, however spontaneous they may seem to be, lack spiritual meaning and authenticity.

Consequently: first of all our meditation should begin with the realization of our nothingness and helplessness in the presence of God. This need not be a mournful or discouraging experience. On the contrary, it can be deeply tranquil and joyful since it brings us in direct contact with the source of all joy and all life. But one reason why our meditation never gets started is perhaps that we never make this real, serious return to the center of our own nothingness before God. Hence we never enter into the deepest reality of our relationship with him.

In other words we meditate merely "in the mind," in the imagination, or at best in the desires, considering religious truths from a detached objective viewpoint. We do not begin by seeking to "find our heart," that is to sink into a deep awareness of the ground of our identity before God and in God. "Finding our heart" and recovering this awareness of our inmost identity implies the recognition that our external, everyday self is to a great extent a mask and a fabrication. It is not our true self. And indeed our true self is not easy to find. It is hidden in obscurity and "nothingness," at the center where we are in direct dependence on God. But since the reality of all Christian meditation depends on this recognition, our attempt to meditate without it is in fact self-contradictory. It is like trying to walk without feet.

Another consequence: even the capacity to recognize our condition before God is itself a grace. We cannot always attain it at will. To learn meditation does not, therefore, mean learning an artificial technique for infallibly producing "compunction" and the "sense of our nothingness" whenever we please. On the contrary, this would be the result of violence and would be inauthentic. Meditation implies the capacity to receive this grace whenever God wishes to grant it to us, and therefore a permanent disposition to humility, attention to reality, receptivity, pliability. To learn to meditate then means to gradually get free from habitual hardness of heart, torpor and grossness of mind, due to arrogance and non-acceptance of simple reality, or resistance to the concrete demands of God's will.

If in fact our hearts remain apparently indifferent and cold, and we find it morally impossible to "begin" meditating in this way, then we should at least realize that this coldness is itself a sign of our need and of our helplessness. We should take it accordingly as a motive for prayer. We might also reflect that perhaps without meaning to we have fallen into a spirit of routine, and are not able to see how to recover our spontaneity without God's grace, for which we must wait patiently, but with earnest desire. This waiting itself will be for us a school of humility.

Reprinted by permission from Thomas Merton, *The Climate of Monastic Prayer* (Cistercian Publications, 1969), 94-98. [This also appears as *Contemplative Prayer* (N.Y.: Image Books, 1969), 68-71.].

Unless the Christian participates to some degree in the dread, the sense of loss, the anguish, the dereliction and the destitution of the Crucified, he cannot really enter into the mystery of the liturgy. He can neither understand the rites and prayers, nor appreciate the sacramental signs and enter deeply into the grace they mediate. Father Monchanin has wisely observed the emptiness of a certain superficial optimism which freely distributes clichés about the "sense of history" and evades the reality of dread by plunging into ceaseless and generally useless activity. They prove themselves to be blind agents, he says, by the very emptiness of their efforts. "For us," Fr. Monchanin continues, "let it be enough to know ourselves to be in the place God wants for us (in the modern world) and carry on our work, even though it be no more than the work of an ant, infinitesimally small, and with unforeseeable results. Now is the hour of the garden and the night, the hour of silent offering: therefore the hour of hope: God alone. Faceless, unknown, unfelt, yet undeniable: God."(*Ecrits Spirituels*, 126)

Let us frankly recognize the true import and the true challenge of the Christian message. The whole gospel kerygma becomes impertinent and laughable if there is an easy answer to everything in a few external gestures and pious intentions. Christianity is a religion for men who are aware that there is a deep wound, a fissure of sin that strikes down to the very heart of man's being. They have tasted the sickness that is present in the inmost heart of man estranged from his God by guilt, suspicion and covert hatred. If that sickness is an illusion, then there is no need for the Cross, the sacraments and the Church. If the Marxists are right in diagnosing this human dread as the expression of guilt and inner dishonesty of an alienated class, then there is no need to preach Christ any more, and there is no need either of liturgy or of meditation. History has yet to show the Marxists are right in this matter however, since by advancing on their own crudely optimistic assumptions they have unleashed a greater evil and a more deadly falsity in man's murderous heart than anyone except the Nazis. And the Nazis, in their turn, borrowed from Nietzsche a similar false diagnosis of the Christian's "fear of the Lord." It is nevertheless true that the spirit of individualism, associated with the culture and economy of the West in the Modem Age, has had a disastrous effect on the validity of Christian prayer. But what is meant by individualism in the life of prayer?

The interior life of the individualist is precisely the kind of life that closes in on itself without dread, and rests in itself with more or less permanent satisfaction. It is to some extent immune to dread, and is able to take the inevitable constrictions and lesions of an inner life complacently enough, spiriting them away with devotional formulas. Individualism in prayer is content precisely with the petty consolations of devotionalism and sentimentality. But more than that, individualism resists the summons to communal witness and collective human response to God. It shuts itself up and hardens itself against everything that would draw it out of itself. It refuses to participate in what is not immediately pleasing to its limited devotional tastes here and now. It remains centered and fixed upon a particular form of consolation which is either totally intimate or at best semi-private, and prefers this to everything else precisely because it need not and cannot be shared.

The purpose of this fixation (which can be maintained with a stubborn will and a minimum of faith) is to produce reassurance, a sense of spiritual identity, an imaginary fulfillment, and perhaps even an excuse for evading the realities of life.

It is unfortunately all too true that bogus interiority has saved face for pious men and women who were thus preserved from admitting their total non-entity. They have imagined that they were capable of love just because they were capable of devout sentiment. One aspect of this convenient spiritual disease is its total insistence on ideals and intentions, in complete divorce from reality, from act, and from social commitment. Whatever one interiorly desires, whatever one dreams, whatever one imagines: that is the beautiful, the godly and the true. Pretty thoughts are enough. They substitute for everything else, including charity, including life itself.

It is precisely the function of dread to break down this glass house of false interiority and to deliver man from it. It is dread, and dread alone, that drives a man out of this private sanctuary in which his solitude becomes horrible to himself without God. But without dread, without the disquieting capacity to see and to repudiate the idolatry of devout ideas and imaginings, man would remain content with himself and with his inner life in meditation, in liturgy or in both. Without dread, the Christian cannot be delivered from the smug self-assurance of the devout ones who know all the answers in advance, who possess all the clichés of the inner life and can defend themselves with infallible ritual forms against every risk and every demand of dialogue with human need and human desperation.

This individualist piety is then a poor substitute for true personalism. It robs man of the power to put himself free, without care, at the disposal of other persons (the *disponibilité* of Gabriel Marcel). But only this freedom of self-disposal in openness, without afterthought, can enable man to find himself as a person. It is precisely this freedom, this openness, which is essential for fully mature participation in liturgical worship. This power of self-surrender is not gained except through the experience of that dread which afflicts us when we taste the awful dereliction of the soul closed in upon itself. . .

A dread that would merely thrust a man deeper into himself and into supposed contemplation is not yet serious. The only full and authentic purification is that which turns a man completely inside out, so that he no longer has a self to defend, no longer an intimate heritage to protect against imagined inroads and dilapidations.

Reprinted by permission from *The Climate of Monastic Prayer by* Thomas Merton, copyright © Cistercian Publications, 1969, 143-147. [This also appears as *Contemplative Prayer*, N.Y.: Image Books, 1969, 106-109.].

[Here Merton links person with God's creative love.]

If we take a . . . living and . . . Christian perspective we find in our-selves a simple affirmation which is not of ourselves. It simply is. In our being there is a primordial yes that is not our own; it is not at our own disposal; it is not accessible to our inspection and understanding; we do not even fully experience it as real (except in rare and unique circumstances). And we have to admit that for most people this pri-mordial "yes" is something they never advert to at all. It is in fact abso-lutely unconscious, totally forgotten.

Basically, however, my being is not an affirmation of a limited self, but the "yes" of Being itself, irrespective of my own choices. Where do "I" come in? Simply in uniting the "yes" of my own freedom with the "yes" of Being that already is before I have a chance to choose. This is not "adjustment." There is nothing to adjust. There is reality, and there is free consent. There is the actuality of one "yes." In this actuality no question of "adjustment" remains and the ego vanishes.

From *Conjectures of a Guilty Bystander* by Thomas Merton, N.Y.: Image Books, 1968, 266.

Who am I? My deepest realization of who I am is-I am one loved by Christ. This is a very important conception. It takes us below the mere level where I decide who I am by the reaction of persons to me. On the social level we create identities for one another by the way we treat each other. If you treat a sister as a difficulty person you make her a difficulty person . . . expectations of other people are secondary. . . The depths of our identity is in the center of my being where I am known by God. I know He sees me. I am glad He sees me and His seeing is love and mercy and acceptance. The great central thing in Christian Faith and Hope is the courage to realize oneself and to accept oneself as loved by God even though one is not worthy. Identity does not consist in creating worthiness, because He loves us in any way. We know God loves us as we are.

From Thomas Merton, "A Conference on Prayer, Calcutta, October 27, 1968." *Sisters Today*, vol. 41(April 1970), 456.

IX. Revelation Selections

[Avery Dulles has written extensively about revelation, and the excerpts from the following article highlight the important distinction between the subjective and objective understandings of revelation.]

The Problem of Revelation

Regarding the basic meaning of the term "revelation" there is a fair degree of consensus in our time. The term may be defined either phenomenologically or theologically. Phenomenologically, it signifies a sudden or unexpected disclosure of a deeply meaningful truth or reality. Revelation usually connotes that the new awareness or knowledge comes upon one as a gift, that it answers a real need, and that it effects a wonderful transformation in the recipient.

Theologically, revelation signifies an action, of God, by which he makes known himself or something he intends to manifest. The theological notion of revelation presupposes or at least implies, that God exists and has dealings with the world. Divine revelation, according to Christian theologians, is a gift; it answers a real need-delivery from darkness and death-and makes a profound difference, inasmuch as it "justifies" or "saves" those who would otherwise perish. Christians believe that God's revealing action undergirds the faith of ancient Israel and that of the Christian Church. The Bible, which expresses this historical faith, is accordingly viewed as a primary document of revelation.

Notwithstanding these basic agreements there is no consensus among Christian or Catholic theologians as to the forms in which revelation comes, where it is principally found, or how it is related to faith. In the present paper I shall seek to classify and evaluate some of the most prominent modern theories.

My own concern is with the logical schematization of positions, but in order to give concreteness and actuality to the analysis I shall take the risk of naming some authors as representatives of the various points of view. In so doing I am not seeking to pass judgment on any author, and I gladly recognize that most authors are too complex in their thinking to fit neatly into one or another of my pigeon holes.

A. Objectivist or Intellectualist Theories

In some theologies of revelation the accent is placed primarily on the revealed datum as a divinely revealed datum as a divinely given truth that can be conceptually known, formulated in human language and passed on by speech and writing. These objectivist or intellectualist views of revelation may be divided into two subcategories according to whether revelation is thought to be given primarily in propositions or in historical events.

1. Propositional Theories

The propositional theory of revelation is so familiar to most Catholics that a very brief description will suffice. In this theory human knowledge is sharply divided into two kinds-revealed and acquired. Revealed knowledge is a gift; it descends from on high, and man receives it passively. Acquired knowledge is achieved through an exercise of man's natural powers; in an ascending movement he actively lays hold of the truth.

Revelation according to this theory is initially given to certain privileged recipients, to whom the word of God comes directly. This occurs in two distinct ways: prophetic and apostolic. Prophets receive the word of God as an interior gift. Concepts and judgments are directly infused into their mind from on high. The apostles initially receive the word of God directly from Jesus Christ and then, through further inspirations of the Holy Spirit, penetrate more deeply the meaning of Christ's message. Revelation, having been received by the prophets and apostles, is then handed down in Scripture and tradition, which constitute the written and oral vehicles of the word of God. Such, in outline, is the view of revelation set forth by Francis Suarez. With some qualifications this view may be said to correspond to the statements of the Council of Trent (DS 1501) and of the first Vatican Council (DS 3004, 3006, 3011).

Although still maintained by many theologians whose ideas were formed before Vatican Council II, the propositional theory of revelation has been under steadily increasing pressure from exegetes and theologians. Biblical scholarship has reached a virtual consensus that the prophets, the apostles. And Jesus himself did not arrive at their insights solely through miraculously infused knowledge, but that they relied heavily on experience and personal efforts. The Holy Spirit assisted the prophets, but did not prevent them from being conditioned by their historical situation.

In its treatment of mediate revelation, the propositional stance, neglects the religious dimension of the assent of faith. As many Thomistic theologians have objected, faith goes out, in the first instance, not to the content of abstract statements but to God as a concrete and personal reality grasped with the help of such statements. For revelation to have the saving value attributed to it by the biblical and Christian tradition it must make a profound impact on the believer as subject; it must make God and his saving activity concretely present. In the propositional theory, mediate revelation appears not as the self-disclosure of the living God but as a collection of human statements about God. The biblical term being "word of God" is distorted by being understood too intellectualistically, too abstractly. The healing and transforming dimension of God's word is treated as if it were separable from revelation itself.

2. Event Theories

In an attempt to get away from the excessively verbal and abstract presentation of revelation in the propositional theory, an increasing number of theologians in the 1940's and 1950's turned to the facts of history, and especially the history of Israel recounted in the Bible, as the primary locus of revelation. Revelation according to this theory consists primarily in God's action in history and secondarily in the divinely guaranteed record and interpretation of that action. This basic position, previously set forth by William Temple, George Ernest Wright, and others, is today most stoutly defended by Wolfhart Pannenberg and a small circle of theologians associated with him.

Pannenberg and his associates contend that there is no direct self-communication of God either through infused ideas or through divinely given words. God makes himself known indirectly through the mighty acts by which he exhibits his lordship over history. Pannenberg insists on the self-evidencing character of the historical events as known by the recipient of revelation-events that can be reconstructed by objective scholarship. Historical revelation, he asserts, is "no secret or mysterious happening" but is "open to anyone who has eyes to see." In contrast to many exponents of "salvation history" Pannenberg asserts that the words of Scripture and tradition add nothing to the inherent intelligibility of the events themselves, provided these are viewed in their full historical context. Ultimately, he points out, the full context must include not only the immediate significance of the events but also their extended causal efficacy within the framework of universal history.

While this equation of revelation with historical events has attracted considerable interest, it has not won a wide following in either Protestant or Catholic circles. In Protestantism opposition has come from conservative evangelicals, who reject a critical approach to the Bible, and from Lutherans and Calvinists, who insist on the primacy of faith over reason. Barthians, Bultmannians, and post-Bultmannians find that Pannenberg neglects the efficacy of the proclaimed word.

Catholics have been attracted by the efforts of Pannenberg to overcome the dualism between faith and reason, but they have been bothered by Pannenberg's naturalistic conception of reason. Omitting other criticisms, we may here concentrate on two. First, the theory of historiography behind Pannenberg's work, especially his early work, overlooks the subjective input of the historian in the selection and interpretation of the data. Pannenberg seems to presuppose a historian whose point of view is entirely determined by the events themselves as perceived in their historical context. A neutral or unconcerned historian, as Pannenberg's critics remark, could never find revelation in history.

This brings us to the second criticism. Pannenberg considers that man's natural powers, without any special assistance, suffice for the appropriation of revelation. Revelation, he contends, can be recognized by those who have no faith. In his insistence that reason can cogently demonstrate the fact of revelation, Pannenberg exposes himself to the suspicion of accepting rationalism akin to that of the nineteenth-century German Catholic, Georg Hermes. This position, according to some scholars, is contrary to the Bible.

3. Event-plus-Word Theories

Dissatisfied with the theories that would place revelation simply in words or simply in historical events, some theologians have attempted a combination of the two preceding theories. Toward the end of the nineteenth century, J. B. Franzelin, relying on the earlier work of John de Lugo, wrote that "God actually speaks not by words alone but by the whole complex of his words and deeds." The word of God in its totality thus consists of both formal words (written or spoken) and significant actions. The words announce the truth; the deeds authenticate the words as divine and revealed.

In our own century this theory has been developed with rather more emphasis on the value of deeds as inherently significant. Edward

Schillebeeckx holds that the word of God in the Old Testament consists in God's salutary, actions in history as "clarified by word of the prophet, in whom this action and dialogue have found a clear response." So in the New Testament, according to Schillebeeckx, the words of Jesus and of the apostles complement the human actions of Jesus (which may be called words in a wider sense, since they communicate his mind and spirit) and thus constitute them as revelation.

Rene Latourelle adopts a similar position, except that he seems to distinguish more sharply between word and deed. He holds that the works of God in salvation history are not revelation apart from the divinely given word of testimony that accompanies them. God's word comes first to the prophet in the form of an interior revelation enabling the prophet to understand the historical event. Then the prophet by speech or writing presents the event and its meaning as objects of divine testimony. Events such as the Exodus and the Cross, apart from the divine or prophetic word, would not be revelation, but, accompanied by such a word, would become revelation.

The basic position of these authors can claim some support from Vatican II's *Dei verbum*, which declares:

> This plan of revelation is realized by deeds and words, having an inner unity: the deeds wrought by God in the history of salvation manifest and confirm the teaching and realities signified by the words, while the words proclaim the deeds and clarify the mystery contained in them.

This compromise position escapes some of the difficulties involved in each of the two preceding theories taken alone. The deed-element lends concreteness and credibility, to what would otherwise be an excessively abstract and authoritarian view of revelation; the word-element provides a means of overcoming the ambiguity of the events of salvation history. But as long as word and deed are seen as two parallel, disconnected, and complementary forms of revelation, the theory remains unsatisfactory. If the events themselves convey no clear significance, how can an authoritative declaration make them clear? Must we not say that in the last analysis revelation is communicated only by the words? We seem, then, to be ultimately thrown back on an infused knowledge for which only the prophet can vouch. This is to incur the risks and improbabilities associated with the propositional theory of revelation as noted above.

B. Personalist and Existential Theories

The traditional theories of revelation thus far described may be characterized as objectivist. They define revelation almost entirely from the point of view of God rather than that of the believing subject. The revealed datum is constituted by God alone, who then miraculously transmits it to his human messengers. The necessity of faith is explained not in terms of its intrinsic relationship to man's needs, but rather in terms of man's extrinsic obligation to accept whatever it may please God to assert.

In the twentieth century, both Protestants and Catholics have turned sharply against the objectivist view of revelation. The new trend was remotely prepared for by Luther, to whom faith came as delivery from a deep existential anxiety. Some nineteenth-century German philosophers, such as Kant, Fichte, and Feuerbach, emphasized the contribution of the knowing subject to the content of his knowledge. Influenced by idealism, some German theologians of the nineteenth and early twentieth centuries (Schliermacher, Otto, Troeltsch) began to look upon revelation as necessarily correlative with man's innate religious sensibilities. Others (Kierkegaard, Barth), while vigorously denying that man has any antecedent capacity for revelation, strongly asserted that revelation, when it comes, has a profound salutary impact, destroying man's self-reliance and giving him confident reliance on God. All these tendencies have in common a new interest in the believer as subject. They may be called "subjectivist" or, to use a term less tainted with pejorative connotations, personalist.

1. Kerygmatic Theology

Protestants such as Barth and Bultmann, followed in part by Catholics such as Jungmann and Lakner, identified revelation, very closely with the kerygma-that is to say, with the proclamation of God's mighty deeds in Jesus Christ. This kerygmatic theology had a strongly existential quality because it saw the kerygma as intimately related to human experience to the demands of Christian living.

In Bultmann the existential dimension becomes particularly strong because revelation is identified with the event that occurs here and now when the message of the Cross and Resurrection is preached. This message summons man to decision and authentic existence today: it opens man's eyes to his own status before God and enables him to actualize the authentic possibilities of his existence. Bultmann is emphatic in holding that revelation consists only in this transforming impact; it does not rest upon scientifically authenticated historical information or involve abstract doctrinal truth.

Bultmann's position, as is well known, has been attacked from two sides. On the one hand, traditionally oriented theologians, such as Barth, Cullmann, and most Catholic critics, complain that he arbitrarily reduces revelation to what contemporary man finds existentially meaningful. On the other hand, personalistic and humanistic theologians tend to find Bultmann's idea of the kerygma too authoritarian and too dogmatic. Karl Jaspers, for instance, protests that Bultmann's insistence on justification by faith alone makes his position "altogether orthodox and illiberal, despite his liberalism as a man and as a historian."

Bultmann's contemporary disciples generally mitigate their master's sharp antithesis between faith and history, but they retain his concern for the existential impact of the message. There is no revelation, they insist, unless God's word encounters me today in an event that transforms my personal existence. In bringing out this dynamic aspect of Christian revelation, the Bultmannians have made an invaluable contribution, much appreciated by some Catholics.

2. Karl Rahner

In twentieth-century Catholic theology there has been a concern for the subjective dimension parallel to that just noted in Protestantism. At the turn of the century the Modernists rebelled against the and abstractions of scholastic theology and sought, as had Schleiermacher, to connect revelation with religious experience. The Idealism of Kant and Fichte made a profound impression on Catholic philosophers such as Maurice Blondel and Joseph Marechal, who introduced a "Copernican revolution" into Catholic thinking. In the theology of Karl Rahner, Marechal's transcendental Thomism joins hands with an existential philosophy derived, like Bultmann's, from Heidegger.

Rahner's theology of revelation, which has profoundly influenced almost the whole Catholic theological scene, is rooted in a vision of man as a subject who constantly reaches out toward an infinite that evades grasp. Man's exigency for the divine, combined with his incapacity to seize it, provides a point of insertion for revelation. The call of grace renders man positively restless for an experience of communion with God. To satisfy this call to eternal life, God makes himself

present to every man; he offers himself in love to those who freely open themselves to the leading of grace.

According to Rahner, therefore, grace is offered to every human person. Grace, moreover, is not a merely objective or ontic reality. As the presence of God himself to the human spirit, grace has a profound transforming impact on man's outlook (his "horizon"). For this reason grace itself may in some sense be called "revelation." Revelation, for Rahner, does not consist primarily in external historical phenomena or in reports concerning another world. It is not given first of all in words, concepts, and propositions, but rather in a change of horizon. The shift of horizon effected by divine grace is, in Rahner's vocabulary, transcendental revelation.

Unlike Bultmann, Rahner does not deny that revelation is also given in historical events and propositional teaching. But these determinate forms of revelation are in his theology secondary. They result from the transcendental revelation constituted by grace. Once grace has been given and accepted into the inner life of the person, it inevitably tends to exteriorize itself in the believer's ideas, statements, and behavior. The reflexive thematization of transcendental revelation results in what Rahner calls "predicamental revelation."

The record of progressive exteriorization of revelation in human history, speaks significantly to the believer in so far as that history symbolically expresses fundamentally the same life of grace that is occurring within each individual. The person and career of Jesus constitute, for Rahner, the supreme expression of God's loving gift of himself and of creation's loving response. Since Christ is the unsurpassable point of meeting between God and man, between grace and nature, he is the high point both of transcendental and of predicamental revelation. He represents the asymptotic limit of the union with God to which all men are called. To discover Christ as the focus of salvation history is therefore to achieve a new level of self-understanding.

Rahner's theology of revelation, because it makes ample provision for existential and experiential factors, has had enormous influence on other Catholic theologians. . .

Mediating Theories

The objectivist theories place all the initiative on the side of God, who is regarded as delivering a formulated message or at least as expressing himself with full clarity by miraculous deeds that could bear only a single interpretation. Faith is represented as a merely passive

reception of a previously determinate "word of God." The personalist
or subjectivist theories, on the other hand, attribute revelation, as a
formulated message, to the dynamism of the human spirit embodying
its own inner faith-experience in an appropriate symbolic form.

Between these two opposed tendencies there is a large stream of contemporary theology, with which I align myself, that situates revelation
and faith in a dialogical interaction, wherein the believer responds creatively to the self-manifestation of God, not simply in the depths of his
own subjectivity, but in the cosmos and history. According to this third
school of thought, revelation is neither an external datum that imposes
itself on any sane and honest observer-as in the first theory-nor a free
expression of one's own subjectivity-as in the second-but a disciplined
response that unfolds under the aegis of faith within a community and a
tradition. . .

From Avery Dulles, "The Problem of Revelation," *Proceedings of the Catholic
Theological Society* 1974, reprinted by permission of the author and of the
Catholic Theological Society of America, 77-86, 97-98.

*[Hans Urs von Balthasar is one of the great theologians of the late
twentieth century whose writing, when not polemical reflects the depth
of contemplative tradition.]*

The majesty of this absolute love-the central phenomenon of revela-
tion-is the source of every form of authority possessed by the mediators
between man and God. The primal authority is possessed neither by
the Bible (the written "Word of God"), nor by the kerygma (the living
proclamation of the "Word of God"), nor in ecclesiastical office (the
official representative of the "Word of God")-all three are 'only' word
and not yet flesh; the Old Testament too as "word" is only moving towards ultimate authority-the primal authority is the Son interpreting the
Father through the Holy Spirit as divine love. For it is only at the
source of revelation that authority (or majesty)-and love coincide. All
an authoritative call to submissive faith in revelation can do is to pre-
pare men to see the love of God made manifest, and help them to value
that love fittingly.

Divine love may give itself with such overwhelming power that man
perceives nothing but the crushing majesty of the Glory, and his response is concentrated into a single answer, utter obedience; but both

word and answer derive their meaning from the fact that the eternal Person has given himself a finite person in such a way that the possible answer is included in the very act of that giving, whose heart and essence is love.

When faced with the majesty of absolute love, which in revealing itself comes to meet man, brings him back, invites him in and raises him to an inconceivable intimacy, it begins to dawn on man's finite spirit what is really meant by saying that God is the totally-other, "incomprehensible, essentially different from the world, in and of himself most blessed and unspeakably exalted above everything else which can be thought of" (Vatic. I, s. 3, c. i). Without this revelation of love, negative theology becomes so empty of meaning that it is ever in danger of drifting into atheism or agnosticism or into a philosophy (or mysticism) of identity. It is here, nevertheless, where the figure of revelation remains incomprehensible unless it is interpreted in terms of God's love, that the totally-other, the ever-greater, appears and seizes hold of us in the very act of overwhelming us through the ultimately incomprehensible character of that love. Precisely when the creature sees and feels himself drawn towards the heart of God, he sees clearly the irrevocable and inescapable nature of that primary, universally valid relationship between the relative and absolute, worldly and divine being. And he can only endure this frightening shaking of the foundations of his finite being when he has learnt to decipher the figure of revelation-not formally as a "word," but really, as absolute love. That is the language of the New Testament: love is not just one of the divine attributes, any more than man's answering love is one of the Virtues.

From *Love Alone: The Way of Revelation* by Hans Urs von Balthasar London: Sheed and Ward, 1977, reprinted by permission of Burns & Oates, 47-49.

X. Jesus Selections

[Balthasar offers a traditional yet contemplative understanding of Jesus.]

Love as Revelation

If revelation were not love, then a purely receptive attitude to things as they happen would be inhuman and unworthy of God; such an attitude is intelligible only if this rejection of all self-knowledge is to further openness to an experience of transcendent love (as faith). Even God's revelation itself could not instill such an attitude in man as an answer to his word. Love can, a priori (and thus as faith), only be in agreement with love-not with non-love. But what we have learnt about the Word from considering man's answer in fact presupposes what we have learnt from God's word about that answer: Only because the Word, as love, has already been spoken and understood, can man give a loving answer, an answer which simply means making a "free passage" for the Word; it is creation's nihil obstat to God whose desire is to penetrate into a realm where everything is an obstacle to him and contradicts his love.

The proposition "only love can be believed" must now be considered (a) positively and (b) negatively, in the light of the content of the Bible. (a)The life of Jesus was, at first, a life of teaching (the doctrine being clarified in imaginative parables and miracles) and finally, a life of suffering unto death. But the blazing, absolute character of the teaching, that shines in everything he said, promised and demanded, can only be understood if the whole movement of his life is seen to be towards the Cross, so that the words and deeds are validated by the Passion, which explains everything and makes everything possible. If one interprets the Passion as a subsequent catastrophe produced by some accident, every word, not excluding the Sermon on the Mount, becomes unintelligible. It is quite impossible to establish a distinction between a doctrine taught by Jesus before the Passion, with no relation to it, and a teaching put into his mouth after the Passion. The intelligible content (the *Logos*) of the teaching and of everything he did can only be read in the light of "his hour," the hour he waited for, the "baptism" he longed for; in the light of that event in which he fulfilled his prophetic mission and the Old, Jewish Covenant-the mission which culminated in the sacrifice and the supper of the New Covenant.

The whole purpose of Jesus' teaching, whether direct or indirect, is this self-sacrifice, for "his friends" (John 15:13), for "the many" (Matt. 10: 28; Mark 10: 45), for ""all" (John 12:32; 17: 21), and what is more in the particular form that he gave to it. It is not an isolated human achievement; it presents itself to us as an act of obedience, and as the aim of a life spent in self-effacing service to all men (Luke 22:27; John 13:3-I7). The *Logos* and logic of his teaching is drawn from his sacrificial death, and it thus places all his followers-their existence as a whole-under the same sign, the *Logos* of the Cross (1Cor.1:18), so that, by implication, every *Logos* and logic would be annulled (since this logic places life under the law of death) unless it is assumed that Jesus' death, which commands his whole life, is, as such, in his final abandonment, the act which reveals "the power and the wisdom of God" (1Cor.1: 24). But the "power and the wisdom" do not "withhold themselves" (Phil.2: 6), they are poured out to the very end in "weakness" and "folly" precisely as functions of absolute love, "stronger than the strength of man" and "wiser than the wisdom of man" (1 Cor.1: 25).

From *Love Alone The Way of Revelation* by Hans Urs von Balthasar London: Sheed and Ward, 1977, reprinted by permission of Burns & Oates, 68-69.

[Schillebeeckx informs his reflections on the Death of Jesus with New Testament Scholarship.]

A. God's Message in Jesus

From a historical standpoint it is impossible to determine whether a human being bound by time and history has a universal significance, universal and definitive for all human beings. But signs and traces of this, calling for some identification and interpretation on the part of others, must be given, of course, within our human compass of understanding if what is said about Jesus' unique universality is not to be ideological. Jesus of Nazareth must at least have been manifest in history as being, in respect of man's definitive salvation or final good, a catalysing question - an invitation. Christians have interpreted that question and invitation in a very specific way: they have found the definitive promise of salvation and liberation imparted by God in Jesus and so have had reason enough to commend him to others, and thus to witness to Jesus Christ. This has been going on right up to the present day; so that we too are confronted now with the possibility of the catalysing question and invitation that Jesus is; but . . . in an entirely new situation: for us Jesus raises the issue of God in an age which in most if not all sectors of its life appears to do without God. The issue that arises out of Jesus cannot be the assertion, whether justifiable or not, that Jesus is the historical embodiment of an existential message or critique of society. For such a message we of the twentieth century have less and less need to look back to someone who lived in the first century of our era - whyever should we? The historical Jesus a person who still faces us with the question whether the reality of God is not the most important thing in the life of man, a question which, given a positive answer, demands of us a radical metanoia: a reorientating of our own lives. That is why the question which Jesus continues to put to us is in the first instance fundamentally disorientating.

In a modern situation particularly we do well to recognize the distinction between Jesus of Nazareth as being this catalysing question and invitation, and the Christological answer given by the Christian churches to the question. This is also, it seems to me, a consequence of the new pastoral situation in which we are living: namely, that (besides ourselves acknowledging and celebrating the salvation found to be imparted by God in Jesus) we contrive in our proclamation (as well in Christology) to present Jesus as first and foremost a question catalysing what are the problems of our most deeply human, personal and social life. The earthly Jesus was precisely, in fact, someone who in specific, historically very localized circumstances raised the issue of taking a stand for him or against him. Jesus himself never directly answers the question of who he is. His personal identity is as it were woven into his message, way of life and death. Therefore the question raised for us by his message, ministry and death can only be fully answered by making a response to the person of Jesus. Like every other historical occurrence the earthly Jesus did after all share in the ambiguity of history, needing to be interpreted and identified.

In Jesus we are confronted with someone who out of his personal *Abba* experience makes us an assured promise of a "future with and from God" and in his ministry actually proffers it. Apart from the reality of this very original *Abba* experience his message is an illusion, a vacuous myth. To put one's trust in Jesus is to ground oneself in what was named as the ground of Jesus' experience: the Father. It entails recognizing the authentic non-illusory reality of Jesus' *Abba* experience. This recognition is alone possible in an act of believing trust which, although not deriving from rational motives, can yet adduce sufficient rational motives for us to describe such believing trust as

humanly and morally not unjustified. The "historical Jesus" allows of
the Christian response as an interpretation which because of ambiguity
of everything historical is never necessary but is rationally and morally
justified, recognizable in the historical phenomenon, but in itself going
beyond rational motives without excluding them.

[The Death of Jesus]

The gospels would seem to suggest that Jesus was not himself all that
certain of the success which the disciples who had been sent out - two
by two - were able to report to their Master concerning their missionary
journeys. On their return there is detectable in the gospels an at first
gentle but then very plain insistence on Jesus' part that his disciples
should have a "rest" (Mk. 6:30-31), far away from the populace (Mt.
14:22; Mk.6:45). So they all go with Jesus across the lake, but even
there, unfortunately, run into a large crowd: "a flock without shep-
herds" the gospels muse (Mk. 6:30-44; 8:1-10; Mt. 14:13-21; 15:32-39;
and Lk. 9:10-17; Jn. 6: 1-15). It is a striking fact that not only do the
four gospels feature this story but two of them even have dual accounts
of what seems to have followed it: Jesus fed the crowd in miraculous
fashion. But especially significant is the comment (Mk. 6:52; 8:17-
18,21) "They did not understand it." On the one hand Jesus offers (a
meal of) fellowship to sinners; on the other they want to proclaim Jesus
king. Jesus' reaction, according to the gospel narrative, is unambigu-
ous: he constrains (as the text has it) his disciples to rest, away from the
multitude. A certain "tendency to isolation," in other words Jesus' de-
termination to keep his more intimate disciples well away from the
enthusiasm of these people, would seem to be intimated to us by these
New Testament passages. At any rate the Marcan tradition is significant: Jesus is obliged, apparently against the wishes of his disciples, to
"constrain" them (for the time being) to quit the stage, to take the boat
back again to the other side - although it was nightfall and a storm was
threatening: Jesus himself withdraws "to a solitary mountain."
After this incident the focus of Jesus' activity switches apparently
from Galilee to Jerusalem - although the connection is difficult to re-
construct, historically speaking. What does become clear is that, according to the gospels, from then on Jesus regards his message as having failed in Galilee and so decides to make for Jerusalem. From that
moment on, the gospels begin to make clear allusions to the path of
suffering set before Jesus, in other words, to his definitive rejection.

This path is described, "typically," of course, as an "exodus," a journey to Jerusalem. Whereas in the first phase of his public ministry Jesus traveled around the country proclaiming the approach of God's rule, now he is shown, according to the gospel record, as making "a journey towards suffering," a journey towards death. This is defined in part, no doubt, by the historical outcome of events; but perhaps also by historical reminiscences of the already admitted fiasco in Galilee.

Although predictions of the Passion in the gospels are certainly not historical reproductions of Jesus' own words, still the question maybe asked whether they are simply *vaticinia ex eventu*, that is, simply projected back from the events of the crucifixion and of Easter. We shall have to consider whether after the fiasco in Galilee the decision to go up to Jerusalem did not turn the prospect of a possible violent death into a potentially concrete experience. In any case Matthew means to identify, with his . . . "from that moment on" (Mt.16:21) - a particular moment in time, a moment at which a caesura is clearly marked out with a "heretofore." Of course it is hard to form a historical judgement as to the chronological exactness of this; the gospels may be a "schematic version" of a historically gradual process which in the end at any rate made Jesus realize that his mission in Galilee had broadly speaking failed and that, convinced of the rightness and urgency of it as he was, he should look for a different outcome, with before him the possibility of total failure. All of this, though showing clear signs of post-Easter reflection, none the less has roots in an earlier period: even before Good Friday Jesus is "the rejected one" and also feels himself to be so on the basis of the historically short "record" of his public career. I believe that F. Muszner is very perceptive when, apropos of Jesus' decision to leave Galilee for Jerusalem, he says: "At first Jesus goes about as the one who offers the eschatological rule of God; then after the offer is rejected by Israel he does so as the one who with the rejection of the offer is himself rejected." Giving historical criticism its full head, the least that one is bound to say on the score of history is that Jesus of Nazareth, despite his awareness of a plain lethal threat posed by "official Jerusalem," nevertheless deliberately and of set purpose made his way to the city of Zion. His purpose in so doing is something we must look at more closely.

B. Jesus in Face of his Approaching Death

. . .There are enough linguistic signals present in the gospels to indicate awareness of the historical distance between the earthly life of Jesus himself and that of the local Christian churches; so that, along with the proclamation of the Church's Easter kerygma, historical recollection of Jesus' days on earth helps to give substance to the four gospels as concretely presented to us.

1. Gradually Increasing Certainty of a Violent Death

One would have to declare Jesus something of a simpleton if it were maintained that he went up from Galilee to Jerusalem in all innocence, without any idea of the deadly opposition he was to encounter there. Every Jew in those days knew that the Romans had the power of crucifixion, Herod Antipas the *ius gladii* - the right to behead someone and the beheading of John the Baptist must have been vividly present to the mind of Jesus; then lastly, the Sanhedrin was empowered to use stoning (see Stephen's martyrdom). None of this, in itself, is either here or there. It is relevant, though, when the question becomes urgent as to whether Jesus was conscious of doing things, committing actions or proclaiming a message which sooner or later would result in an inevitable collision with one or more of those authorities. When we are dealing with a rational and purposeful individual, and not with an unrealistic, fanatical apocalypticist (even they were anything but fanatical in late Judaism), the consciousness of doing or saying something which could and would cause a fundamental conflict with one of those authorities is at the same time a way of deliberately taking upon oneself responsibility for the legal consequences of such behaviour, so let us link up Jesus' activity with the three centres of power that could possibly impose the death penalty on him.

Jesus was known to have been baptized by John the Baptist; and from the time of his public ministry it was rumoured that he was actually Johannes redivivus (Mk. 6:14); furthermore that, in a manner more radical even than the Baptist, he was proclaiming the message of total change in virtue of God's approaching rule, in a way that called for taking sides for or against his person. It would be naive to suppose that Jesus, having witnessed king Herod Antipas' use of the *ius gladii* , in the case of John the Baptist, failed to relate John's ministry to his own. With the Baptist for an example he knew that the sword of Herod as hanging over his head as well. In Mk. 3:6 the "Herodians," to whom Mark nowhere else refers, are a pointer to a historical reminiscence. In short: such a sane and sensible person as Jesus of Nazareth must have definitely reckoned on possible execution by beheading, like John the Baptist.

Was the Sanhedrin with its power to inflict death by stoning a threat to Jesus? Apart from Mt.16:1,6,11,12 and the Gospel of John the Sadducees (strongest party in the Sanhedrin) are not mentioned as opponents of Jesus until the account of the Passion. It is a known fact, on the other hand, that only after the Jewish War (after AD 70) did the Pharisees, who also had a voice in the Sanhedrin, acquire the leading position ascribed to them in the gospels. Evidently, therefore, the New Testament antagonism between Jesus and the Pharisees is up to a point coloured by the later situation of the Church. One may assume that the tension between Jesus and the Sadducees dated from an earlier period than the story of the Passion would suggest. On the other hand, except for Mt. 27:62, the Pharisees are nowhere mentioned in the account of the Passion. Hence one may suspect that the opposition to Jesus came not so much from just one particular group but from the two most important ones at the time: the Pharisees and, especially towards the end, the Sadducees. It is hard to believe that Jesus was so naive as not to have realized that his words and actions were creating an explosive and for him very dangerous situation, bearing in mind the leaders of the Jewish community at that time.

And then, had Jesus anything to fear directly from the Romans? It was of course by the Romans that he was executed, as the nature of his death - by crucifixion - demonstrates, and so on grounds of possible or alleged Zealotic reactions among the people. Jesus needed least of all to take that possibility into consideration, in view of the tenor of his proclamation, which revealed no interest in the problems of the Roman occupation. There was one particular - that is to say, political interpretation of messianism, which admirers certainly attributed to him, within the range of possible situations. There were obviously some ex-Zealots among Jesus' disciples ("Simon, the Zealot," Lk. 6:15 and parallels; Acts 1:13); according to some authorities, who associate "Iscariot" with *sicarius* (dagger-man), Judas is supposed to have belonged to these circles; even *Boanerges*, the sons of thunder, could, it is said, witness to a Zealotic reminiscence. Appearing in Jerusalem with such a following, with at the time - or probably earlier - an incident like the cleansing of the Temple (Mk.11:15-16 and parallels) and the apparently authentic saying of Jesus about "demolishing the Temple" (Mk. 14:5 8 parallel in Mt.; see Jn. 2:19; Mk. 15:29 parallel in Mt.12:6; Acts 6:14 and Mk. 13:2), coming from someone who proclaims the kingly rule of God over Israel, this may appear, directly or, even more, indirectly, after the complaint registered from the Jewish side with the Roman authorities, as provocation and would in any case make the always rebellion-conscious occupying power antagonistic towards anyone who aroused the feelings of the people.

As a matter of history it is clear of course that Jesus' death was in continuity with the reaction to his public ministry, especially having in mind the example of John the Baptist, who was also done away with "for fear of the Romans". As a final effect Jesus' execution is historically explicable "from the interplay of various factors, each of which was dangerous enough in itself." As Jesus was no fanatic - and that is quite certain from what we know about him - then from a particular moment in his career he must have rationally come to terms with the possibility, in the longer term probability and in the end actual certainty of a fatal outcome. This is more or less unanimously agreed nowadays, by exegetes and historians; it is just theologians who are still affected by Bultmann's dictum that we cannot know what Jesus thought about his death and that he may have been steeped in total despair and perplexity because of this surprising turn of events, which had thwarted all his plans. What had been cautiously uttered by Bultmann as a piece of pure speculation has for certain theologians come to be an essential element in their theological thematizing (and thence "popularized" in some quarters). It smacks more of modish ideology and "cashing in" than of historical accuracy.

2. The Unavoidable Question of Jesus' Own Interpretation

Granted Jesus' basic attitude towards the will of God, his Father, the obvious question concerns his existential attitude to what he himself perceived to be the threatening possibility, likelihood, and then certainty of being rejected and executed, whether by the sword - because of Herod's royal prerogative (as with John the Baptist before him) - or by stoning - by virtue of the powers assigned to the Sanhedrin (as later on with Stephen) - or by crucifixion - as for many at that time, the Roman penalty for serious criminal acts or rebellion. That someone like Jesus, who was proclaiming the imminent arrival of God's rule, would have failed to ponder, in some way, so probable and to him so clearly recognizable an outcome of his future life, can be ruled out from the start. It would mean that Jesus' end was in flagrant contradiction to what he had himself been saying about having a radical confidence in God, whatever the empirical and historical circumstances might be. And that was the kernel both of the message and of the behaviour on Jesus' part which flowed from it; for with all this fulfilled, he could still refer to "being an unprofitable servant" (Lk. 17:7-10). To lack entirely, or simply to refrain from entertaining, any moral or religious standpoint in regard to approaching death would in this case be not only myopic but must indicate an incomprehensibly divided personality.

Thus the fact of his approaching death was something that Jesus was bound to integrate into his overall surrender to God, but also reconcile with a conviction as to the urgency of his message. "Not my will but your will be done" (Mk. 14-36c and parallels). Even if this is not a *verbum ipsissimum*, not a historical Jesus-saying, it unmistakably reflects the inner consistency of Jesus' own preaching and personal bearing during his life. But acceptance of God's will and evaluating concretely the point and purpose of what was to happen are not one and the same thing.

There are authentic sayings enough known to us from the life of Jesus that plainly point towards an attitude of "faithfulness unto death". Jesus is turning for support to Israel's sapiential experience and wisdom tradition when he says that "whoever loses his life will save it" (Mk. 8:35 and parallels; see Lk. 17:33 and parallels; 14: 26). We can gather from Jesus' sayings and actions that as soon as death came in prospect he not only contemplated that possibility but, existentially speaking, must have lived with it: he was forced by circumstances to give a place to approaching death in his radical confidence in God. What place?

The rejection of his message and the prospect of his personal rejection could hardly have been felt by Jesus to constitute at the human level and in themselves a meaningful event. (The fact of the calamity and the incomprehensible event of Jesus' death have a profound effect on the reactions in the New Testament, especially in the contrast-scheme.) Jesus himself was faced with the concrete task of reconciling the historical eventuality of his violent death with the assurance of his message about the approaching kingdom of God. Did Jesus simply allow the certainty of his death to take possession of him in uncomprehending, though radical trust in God; or did he come to see in this historical situation some sort of divine plan of salvation, that not only in spite of but perhaps through the very failure within history of his message, through his death, his message would be vindicated divinely and in sovereign freedom? In this "in spite of" or else "thanks" is the key to the whole theological problem.

All the gospels or attestations on the part of the first Christians are quite sure that Jesus went to the cross freely and deliberately. What we have here is post-Easter theological reflection "after the fact". . .

3. The Last Supper: Unshaken Assurance of Salvation When Face to Face with Death

One can hardly maintain that Jesus both willed and sought after his death as the sole possible way of realizing the kingdom of God. There would have been an element of play-acting about his commitment to his message of *metanoia* and the rule of God, if he had thought and known from the very start that salvation would come only in consequence of his death. That death only comes in prospect as a result of his preaching and mode of life, which constituted an offer of salvation, having been rejected. This is not rescinded or nullified by his death. An opposite interpretation would fail to give full value to Jesus' real function of "pointing the way" by the concrete course of his own life's history; in other words, it disregards the fact of Jesus' "being truly man" in a historical mode. Furthermore, it would simply formalize the actual significance for salvation of Jesus' death.

What can be said on the strength of the real evidence is that at any rate Jesus did nothing to escape a violent death. On the contrary, despite the growing certainty that his message had, broadly speaking, been rejected, he deliberately made for Jerusalem. . .

That the Last Supper was actually a Jewish Passover meal is disputable on many different grounds; so that we shall not consider that aspect here. What is beyond dispute is that a farewell meal was offered by Jesus to his disciples in the consciousness of his impending death. Apropos of this problem we find in the gospels two layers: an older and a more recent one.

The less ancient passages turn out to be liturgical formulae current in the Church as a reminder of what Jesus did during this farewell meal. They contain a recognizable Pauline-cum-Lucan tradition (Lk.22:20a parallel 1 Cor. 11:25) and a Marcan one (Mk. 14:24 parallel Mt. 26:26-28). The Pauline-Lucan tradition might be summarized thus: "This cup, now proffered, affords a share in the new covenant promised by the prophets, which comes about thanks to my martyrdom." Within the tradition, "blood" in this context signifies "the blood of the martyr." In the Marcan tradition, on the other hand, the renewing of the covenant comes about by reason of Jesus' death, interpreted in the light of Exod. 24:8 as a cultic sacrifice: "This is my blood of the covenant."

That these passages have been influenced by liturgical practice in the Church and so have a post-Easter stamp upon them is clear enough. But in both Luke (22:18) and Mark (14:2 5) one can detect an older vein. . .: "Truly I say to you, I shall not drink again of the fruit of the

vine until that day when I drink it new in the kingdom of God"
(Mk.14:25). "From now on I shall not drink of the fruit of the vine
until the kingdom of God comes"(Lk. 22:15-18; see 1 Cor. 11:26). The
passage contains two elements:(1) on the one hand, a main feature of
this meal is the -at any rate- quite emphatic announcement by Jesus of
his imminent death, in other words: this meal is a farewell to all such
earthly fellowship (it really is the very last cup that Jesus will share
with his friends); (2) on the other hand, Jesus offers with it the prospect
of fellowship renewed in the kingdom of God. . . The hard centre of
historical fact is Jesus' explicitly uttered conviction that this is to be the
very last cup he will drink with his disciples in his earthly life; the second element, "until the day when . . ." is secondary. The emphasis is
not on the coming meal but on the "drinking no more" . . . This is most
entitled, historically speaking, to recognition as an intimation of Jesus'
own death. The second clause, "until . . ." has another source: there is
mention elsewhere of the eschatological feast or dinner-party; the combination of the utterance about Jesus' suffering and death with the
glory-to-be is clearly secondary. A prediction regarding the destiny of
the son of man thus becomes at the same time a promise of salvation,
apropos of the future fellowship of the disciples with Jesus.

If the second clause is secondary, what salvific relevance is retained
by the first clause of this old text? Despite Israel's rejection of the last
prophetic offer of salvation made by God, Jesus, face to face with his
coming death, continues to offer his disciples the (last) cup: this shows
Jesus' unshaken assurance of salvation, so that the addition of the "until" clause in Mark and Luke, albeit secondary, is simply a way of making explicit the concrete situation. The renewed fellowship-at-table or
offer of salvation by Jesus to the disciples, in face of approaching
death, still makes perfect sense to Jesus; he has come to proper terms
with his death, which he evidently does not feel to be an absurd miscar-
riage of his mission. Such unassailable religious certainty is surely
food for thought. What does it signify, this conviction on Jesus' part
that his death will be powerless to obstruct the coming rule of God,
which he has proclaimed?

Allowing for the diverse interpretations of the eschatological character of Jesus' message, from his preaching and from his whole attitude to
life this one thing is certain: Jesus stands open to God's future for man
and, on the other hand, his whole life is a service to people, a service of
love. "If anyone would be first, he must be last of all and servant of
all" (Mk. 9:35); this and similar comments (Mt. 7: 12 and parallels;
Mk. 12:33; Lk. 6:27-28), the context of which within the tradition, al-

though worked over later by the Church, is grounded in recollection of
the Last Supper, clearly reflect Jesus' own fundamental attitude to life.
Pro-existence, "being-as-man for the other" and unconditional obedience to God's will, revealed in the Decalogue and in various situations
of man's life, persisted in to the point of death, do indeed evince Jesus'
fidelity to his message, which keeps open God's future, gives God the
final word and makes Jesus persevere in loving service to people, as a
manifestation of God's own benevolence towards them. Even where no
salvific implication is ascribed to Jesus' death in the New Testament, it
is at any rate seen as the "martyr's destiny" of the prophet. . .

. . . there is no getting round the historical fact that in the very face of
death Jesus offers the cup of fellowship to his disciples; this is a token
that he is not just passively allowing death to overcome him but has
actively integrated it into his total mission, in other words, that he understands and is undergoing his death as a final and extreme service to
the cause of God as the cause of men, and that he has communicated
this self-understanding to his intimate disciples under the veiled sign of
extending to them the fellowship-at-table shared with his friends. The
"for you"(*hyper* formula), in the sense of Jesus' whole pro-existence,
had been the historical intention of his whole ministry, which his very
death now substantiates. The crux of the argument - against the back-
ground of Jesus' whole approach to life in loyalty to the Father and in
service to men - is enshrined, it seems to me, in this, that the entire
ministry of Jesus during the period of his public life was not just an
assurance or promise of salvation but a concrete tender of salvation
then and there. He does not just talk about God and his rule; where he
appears he brings salvation and becomes God's rule already realized.
The active acceptance of his own death or rejection can only be understood as Jesus' active incorporation of his death into his mission of offering salvation, and not simply and solely as a "notwithstanding."
This applies with all the greater force because even during his life Jesus' fellowship-at-table shared with sinners was the token of an immediate tender of salvation. Given all this, the fact that it is impossible to
find a *verbim ipsissimum* or authentic saying of Jesus that tells us how
he regarded and evaluated his death (excepting the first section of
Mk.14:25a; Lk. 22:18a) is really irrelevant. Jesus' whole life is the
hermeneusis of his death. The very substance of salvation is sufficiently present in it, which could be and -was in fact articulated later on
in various ways through faith in him. Although the historico-critical
method cannot produce knock-down arguments on this score, still less
can it assert categorically that so far as history goes we do not know

how Jesus understood his own death. Jesus' understanding of that death as part and parcel of his mission of tendering salvation seems to me, therefore, a fact preceding Easter - and demonstrably so, at least for Jesus' self-understanding in the final days of his life. . .

This is a very important conclusion; for it means that even prior to Easter Jesus is saying, in effect at any rate, that the "Jesus affair" is to go ahead. This is not just a vision born of faith and based solely on the disciples' Easter experience; it is his self-understanding that creates the possibility and lays the foundation of the subsequent interpretation by the Christians. There is no gap between Jesus' self-understanding and the Christ proclaimed by the Church. If we ask whether the disciples can be thought to have grasped what Jesus was getting at prior to the whole event of Easter, the answer must be on the negative side. But after the first shock of his dying, the memory of Jesus' life and especially of the Last Supper must have played a vital role in the process of their conversion to faith in Jesus as the Christ, the one imbued to the full with God's Spirit. That Jesus was right in understanding himself thus and was on to the truth when he saw his death as being somehow tied in with his mission to offer salvation cannot of course be legitimated as a fact of history; it can only be dismissed or accepted in faith. But that he did so is a fact of history hard to deny.

[Peter's misunderstanding highlights the difficulty of understanding Jesus' preaching.]

Now they had forgotten to bring bread; and they had only one loaf with them in the boat. 15 And he cautioned them, saying, "Take heed, beware of the leaven of the Pharisees and the leaven of Herod." 16 And they discussed it with one another, 17 saying, "We have no bread . " And being aware of it, Jesus said to them, "Why do you discuss the fact that you have no bread? Do you not yet perceive or understand? Are your hearts hardened? 18 Having eyes do you not see, and having ears do you not hear? And do you not remember? 19 When I broke the five loaves for the five thousand, how many baskets full of broken pieces did you take up?" They said to him, "Twelve." 20 "And the seven for the four thousand, how many baskets full of broken pieces did you take up?" And they said to him, Seven." 21 And he said to them, "Do you not yet understand?"

22And they came to Bethsaida. And some people brought to him a blind man, and begged him to touch him. 23 And he took the blind man by the hand, and led him out of the village; and when he had spit on his eyes and laid his hands upon him, he asked him, "Do you see anything?" 24 And he looked up and said, "I see men; but they look like trees, walking." 25 Then again he laid his hands upon his eyes; and he looked intently and was restored, and saw everything clearly. 26 And he sent him away to his home, saying, "Do not even enter the village."

27 And Jesus went on with his disciples, to the villages of Caesarea Philippi; and on the way he asked his disciples, "Who do men say that I am?" 28And they told him, "John the Baptist; and others say, Eli'jah; and others one of the prophets." 29 And he asked them, "But who do you say that I am?" Peter answered him, "You are the Christ." 30 And he charged them to tell no one about him.

31 And he began to teach them that the Son of man must suffer many things, and be rejected by the elders and the chief priests and the scribes, and be killed, and after three days rise again. 32 And he said this plainly. And Peter took him, and began to rebuke him. 33 But turning and seeing his disciples. he rebuked Peter, and said, "Get behind me, Satan! For you are not on the side of God, but of men."

34 And he called to him the multitude with his disciples, and said to them, "If any man would come after me, let him deny himself and take up his cross and follow me. 35 For whoever would save his life will lose it; and whoever loses his life for my sake and the gospel's will save it. 36For what does it profit a man, to gain the whole world and forfeit his life? 37 For what can a man give in return for his life? 37 For whoever is ashamed of me and of my words in this adulterous and sinful generation, of him will the Son of man also be ashamed, when he comes in the glory of his Father with the holy angels."

From Mark 8

[Jesus as religious reformer comes through most memorably in the sermon on the mount.]

Seeing the crowds, he went up on the mountain, and when he sat down his disciples came to him. 2 And he opened his mouth and taught them, saying:

3 "Blessed are the poor in spirit, for theirs is the kingdom of heaven. 4 "Blessed are those who mourn, for they shall be comforted.

5 "Blessed are the meek, for they shall inherit the earth.

6 "Blessed are those who hunger and thirst for righteousness, for they shall be satisfied.

7 "Blessed are the merciful, for they shall obtain mercy.

8 "Blessed are the pure in heart, for they shall see God.

9 "Blessed are the peacemakers, for they shall be called sons of God.

10 "Blessed are those who are persecuted for righteousness' sake, for theirs is the kingdom of heaven.

11"Blessed are you when men revile you and persecute you and utter all kinds of evil against you falsely on my account. 12 Rejoice and be glad, for your reward is great in heaven, for so men persecuted the prophets who were before you.

13 "You are the salt of the earth; but if salt has lost its taste, how shall its saltness be restored? It is no longer good for anything except to be thrown out and trodden under foot by men. 14 "You are the light of the world. A city set on a hill cannot be hid. 15 Nor do men light a lamp and put it under a bushel, but on a stand, and it gives light to all in the house. 16 Let your light so shine before men, that they may see your good works and give glory to your Father who is in heaven.

17 "Think not that I have come to abolish the law and the prophets; I have come not to abolish them but to fulfill them. 18 For truly, I say to you, till heaven and earth pass away, not an iota, not a dot, will pass from the law until all is accomplished. 19 Whoever then relaxes one of the least of these commandments and teaches men so, shall be called least in the kingdom of heaven; but he who does them and teaches them shall be called great in the kingdom of heaven. 20 For I tell you, unless your righteousness exceeds that of the scribes and Pharisees, you will never enter the kingdom of heaven.

21 "You have heard that it was said to the men of old, 'You shall not kill; and whoever kills shall be liable to judgment.' 22 But I say to you that every one who is angry with his brother' shall be liable to judgment; whoever insults his brother shall be liable to the council, and whoever says, 'You fool!' shall be liable to the hell of fire. 23 So if you are offering your gift at the altar, and there remember that your brother has something against you, 24 leave your gift there before the altar and go; first be reconciled to your brother, and then come and offer your

gift. 25 Make friends quickly with your accuser, while you are going with him to court, lest your accuser hand you over to the judge, and the judge to the guard, and you be put in prison; 26 truly, I say to you, you will never get out till you have paid the last penny.

27 "You have heard that it was said, 'You shall not commit adultery.' 28 But I say to you that every one who looks at a woman lustfully has already committed adultery with her in his heart. 29 If your right eye causes you to sin, pluck it out and throw it away; it is better that you lose one of your members than that your whole body be thrown into hell. 30And if your right hand causes you to sin, cut it off and throw it away; it is better that you lose one of your members than that your whole body go into hell."

31 "It was also said, 'Whoever divorces his wife, let him give her a certificate of divorce.' 32 But I say to you that every one who divorces his wife, except on the ground of unchastity, makes her an adulteress; and whoever marries a divorced woman commits adultery.

33 "Again you have heard that it was said to the men of old, 'You shall not swear falsely, but shall perform to the Lord what you have sworn.' 34 But I say to you, Do not swear at all, either by heaven, for it is the throne of God, or by the earth, for it is his footstool, or by Jerusalem, for it is the city of the great King. 36 And do not swear by your head, for you cannot make one hair white or black. 37 Let what you say be simply 'Yes' or 'No,' anything more than this comes from evil.'

38 "You have heard that it was said, 'An eye for an eye and a tooth for a tooth.' 39 But I say to you, Do not resist one who is evil. But if any one strikes you on the right cheek, turn to him the other also; 40 and if any one would sue you and take your coat, let him have your cloak as well;

41 and if any one forces you to go one mile, go with him two miles. 42 Give to him who begs from you, and do not refuse him who would borrow from you.

43 "You have heard that it was said, 'You shall love your neighbor and hate your enemy.' 44 But I say to you, Love your enemies and pray for those who persecute you, 45 So that you may be sons of your Father who is in heaven; for he makes his sun rise on the evil and on the good, and sends rain on the just and on the unjust. 46 For if you love those who love you, what reward have you? Do not even the tax collectors do the same? 47 And if you salute only your brethren, what more are you doing than others? Do not even the Gentiles do the same? 48 You, therefore, must be perfect, as your heavenly Father is perfect.

Beware of practicing your piety before men in order to be seen by them; for then you will have no reward from your Father who is in heaven.

2 "Thus, when you give alms, sound no trumpet before you, as the hypocrites do in the synagogues and in the streets, that they may be praised by men. Truly, I say to you, they have their reward. 3 But when you give alms, do not let your left hand know what your right hand is doing, 4 So that your alms may be in secret; and your Father who sees in secret will reward you.

5 "And when you pray, you must not be like the hypocrites; for they love to stand and pray in the synagogues and at the street corners-, that they may be seen by men. Truly, I say to you, they have their reward. 6 But when you pray, go into your room and shut the door and pray to your Father who is in secret; and your Father who sees in secret will reward you.

7 "And in praying do not heap up empty phrases as the Gentiles do; for they think that they will be heard for their many words. 8 "Do not be like them, for your Father knows what you need before you ask him. 9 Pray then like this: Our Father who art in heaven, Hallowed be thy name.   10 Thy kingdom come, Thy will be done, On earth as it is in heaven. 11 Give us this day our daily bread;   12 And forgive us our debts, As we also have forgiven our debtors; 13 And lead us not into temptation, But deliver us from evil.

14 For if you forgive men their trespasses, your heavenly Father also will forgive you; 15 but if you do not forgive men their trespasses, neither will your Father forgive your trespasses.

16 "And when you fast, do not look dismal, like the hypocrites, for they disfigure their faces that their fasting may be seen by men. Truly, I say to you, they have their reward. 17 But when you fast, anoint your bead and wash your face, 18 that your fasting may not be seen by men but by your Father who is in secret; and your Father who sees in secret will reward you.

19 "Do not lay up for yourselves treasures on earth, where moth and rust consume and where thieves break in and steal, 20 but lay up for yourselves treasures in heaven, where neither moth nor rust consumes and where thieves do not break in and steal. 21 For where your treasure is, there will your heart be also.

22 "The eye is the lamp of the body. So, if your eye is sound, your whole body will be full of light; 23 but if your eye is not sound, your whole body will be full of darkness. If then the light in you is darkness, how great is the darkness!

24 "No one can serve two masters; for either he will hate the one and love the other, or he will be devoted to the one and despise the other. You cannot serve God and mammon.

25 "Therefore I tell you, do not be anxious about your life, what you shall eat or what you shall drink, nor about your body, what you shall put on. Is not life more than food, and the body more than clothing? 26 Look at the birds of the air: they neither sow nor reap nor gather into barns, and yet your heavenly Father feeds them. Are you not of more value than they? 27 And which of you by being anxious can add one cubit to his span of life? 28 And why are you anxious about clothing? Consider the lilies of the field, how they grow; they neither toil nor spin; 29 yet I tell you, even Solomon in all his glory was not arrayed like one of these. 30 But if God so clothes the grass of the field, which today is alive and tomorrow is thrown into the oven, will he not much more clothe you, 0 men of little faith? 31 Therefore do not be anxious, saying, 'What shall we eat?' or 'What shall we drink?' or 'What shall we wear?' 32 For the Gentiles seek all these things; and your heavenly Father knows that you need them all. 33 But seek first his kingdom and his righteousness, and all these things shall be yours as well.

34 "Therefore do not be anxious about tomorrow, for tomorrow will be anxious for itself. Let the day's own trouble be sufficient for the day.

7:1 Judge not, that you be not judged. 2 For with the judgment you pronounce you will be judged, and the measure you give will be the measure you get. 3 Why do you see the speck that is in your brother's eye, but do not notice the log that is in your own eye? 4 Or how can you say to your brother, 'Let me take the speck out of your eye,' when there is the log in your own eye? 5 You hypocrite, first take the log out of your own eye, and then you will see clearly to take the speck out of your brother's eye.6 "Do not give dogs what is holy; and do not throw your pearls before swine, lest they trample them underfoot and turn to attack you.

7 "Ask, and it will be given you; seek and you will find; knock, and it will be opened to you. 8 For every one who asks receives, and he who seeks finds, and to him who knocks it will be opened. 9 Or what man of you, if his son asks him for a loaf, will give him a stone? 10 Or if he asks for a fish, will give him a serpent? 11 If you then, who are evil, know how to give good gifts to your children, how much more will your Father who is in heaven give good things to those who ask him? 12 So whatever you wish that men would do to you, do so to them; for this is the law and the prophets.

13 "Enter by the narrow gate; for the gate is wide and the way is easy, that leads to destruction, and those who enter by it are many. 14 For the gate is narrow and the way is hard, that leads to life, and those who find it are few.

15 "Beware of false prophets, who come to you in sheep's clothing but inwardly are ravenous wolves. 16 You will know them by their fruits. Are grapes gathered from thorns, or figs from thistles? 17 So, every sound tree bears good fruit, but the bad tree bears evil fruit. 18 A sound tree cannot bear evil fruit, nor can a bad tree bear good fruit. 19 Every tree that does not bear good fruit is cut down and thrown into the fire. 20 Thus you will know them by their fruits.

21 "Not every one who says to me, 'Lord, Lord,' shall enter the kingdom of heaven, but he who does the will of my Father who is in heaven. 22 On that day many will say to me, 'Lord, Lord, did we not prophesy in your name, and cast out demons in your name, and do many mighty works in your name?' 23 And then will I declare to them, 'I never knew you; depart from me, you evildoers.'

24 "Every one then who hears these words of mine and does them will be like a wise man who built his house upon the rock; 25 and the rain fell, and the floods came, and the winds blew and beat upon that house, but it did not fall, because it bad been founded on the rock. 26 And every one who bears these words of mine and does not do them will be like a foolish man who built his house upon the sand; 27 and the rain fell, and the floods came, and the winds blew and beat against that house, and it fell; and great was the fall of it."

28 And when Jesus finished these sayings, the crowds were astonished at his teaching, 29 for he taught them as one who had authority, and not as their scribes.

From Matthew 5-7

INDEX